Measuring National Well-being 2021

Contents

Measuring National Well-being 2021

In replacement of 'Social Trends'

RBWM LIBRARY SERVICES

9580000135777

The data displayed in this document was correct at the time of downloading 26/08/22

Statistical bulletin

Personal and economic well-being in Great Britain: January 2021

Estimates looking across multiple sources for personal and economic well-being to understand the impact of the coronavirus (COVID-19) pandemic on people and households in Great Britain. Covers the period from March 2020 to December 2020.

Contact:
Bella Beynon and Gueorguie Vassilev
PeopleAndProsperity@ons.gov.uk
+44 (0)1633455330 +44 (0)1633 456265

Release date:
21 January 2021

Next release:
To be announced

Correction

9 August 2021 10:00

We have corrected an error in section 3 under the heading Savings, borrowing and affordability. The previous version included details about affordability of an expense and a holiday by age group and parental status, and whether people were able to make ends meet by the same groups. As a result of human error, these groupings were assigned incorrectly, which had a small impact on the proportions quoted. The numbers quoted for the over 60s were most affected by this error, but the overall narrative in this section remains unchanged.

Notice

21 January 2021

Associated data for this statistical bulletin shows total population estimates produced from the Opinions and Lifestyle survey and from the Survey of Living conditions. Additional splits of the from the Opinions and Lifestyle Survey data providing comparable estimates for demographics and personal characteristics, such as age groups, income groups, parental statuses and others, will be released following this publication on 25 January 2020.

Table of contents

1 . Main points

- The labour market shocks associated with the coronavirus (COVID-19) pandemic have been felt more by young people and the lowest paid; people aged under 30 years and those with household incomes under £10,000 were around 35% and 60%, respectively, more likely to be furloughed than the general population.

- Of those who have not been able to work (either because of being on furlough or for another reason), over half (52%) of people in the top income quintile continued to be paid in full, while this was the case for only 28% of those in the lowest income quintile.

- People with a job or seeking work were more likely to have decreased income during the pandemic, and particularly the poorest 20%, while others such as retired people out of the labour market were more protected.

- Throughout the pandemic, employed parents were almost twice as likely to report a reduction in income than the general employed population, although this gap gradually narrowed throughout 2020 as schools reopened.

- Self-employed people were more likely to report reduced working hours and reduced income, even if they had received support from the Self-Employment Income Support Scheme (SEISS).

- By December 2020, nearly 9 million people had to borrow more money because of the coronavirus pandemic; the proportion borrowing £1,000 or more also increased from 35% to 45% since June 2020.

- Impacts to household spending have been felt differently across groups, with parents less able to afford either a holiday or an unexpected but necessary expense than non-parents; they were also roughly 50% more likely to have difficulty meeting their usual expenses.

2 . Work and income

In 2020, the coronavirus (COVID-19) impacted people across all sections of society.

The number of people reporting that they had been furloughed steadily reduced over the summer months, but this proportion started to increase again in November 2020, to coincide with further restrictions across certain parts of the country. Young people and those on the lowest incomes were most likely to be impacted in this second phase of restrictions, as they were in the first lockdown, with a six-fold increase in those aged under 30 years reporting that they had been furloughed. This increased from 2.1% for the five days to 1 November 2020 to 12.3% a week later.

Figure 1: People on lower incomes were more likely to report being furloughed than those on higher incomes

Share of the population reporting that they had been furloughed, by income bracket, Great Britain, 30 April to 20 December 2020

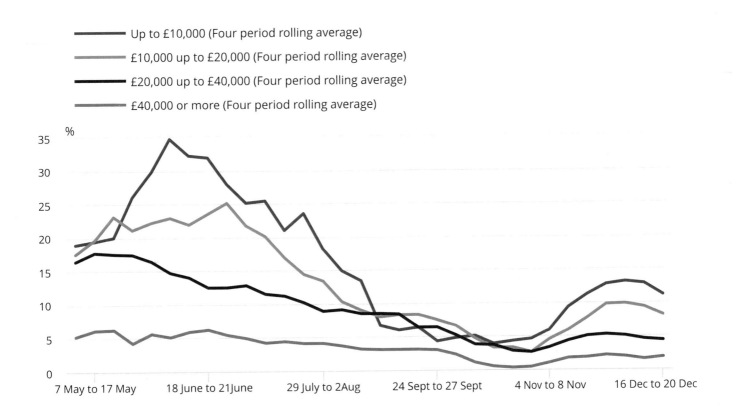

Source: Office for National Statistics – Opinions and Lifestyle Survey

Notes:

1. Responses to the question "In the past seven days, how have your household finances been affected?".

2. Share of respondents who responded "I have been furloughed". This is a self-reported figure, Her Majesty's Revenue and Customs (HMRC) publish official Coronavirus Job Retention Scheme statistics Coronavirus Job Retention Scheme.

3. Four-period rolling average has been calculated.

Those on the lowest incomes were also more likely to be furloughed during 2020. Between 11 and 15 November 2020, when restrictions were tightened in some areas of the country, 17% of people with a household income less than £10,000 reported that they had been furloughed. In comparison, only 2.7% of people with a household income of more than £40,000 reported this.

Similarly, those in high-income groups reported that they were more likely to be able to work from home, with 55.1% of people with income over £20,000 able to work from home compared with 19.1% of people with income less than £20,000.

The Coronavirus Job Retention Scheme allowed employers to "top-up" the earnings of those who were on furlough, and data from the Survey of Living Conditions suggests that this was less likely to happen for those on lower incomes.

Figure 2: People on higher incomes were more likely to be paid in full if they were unable to work, compared with those on lower incomes

Percentage of people responding to whether they were still being paid while their work was on hold, by income quintile band for financial year ending 2020, Great Britain, May 2020 to October 2020

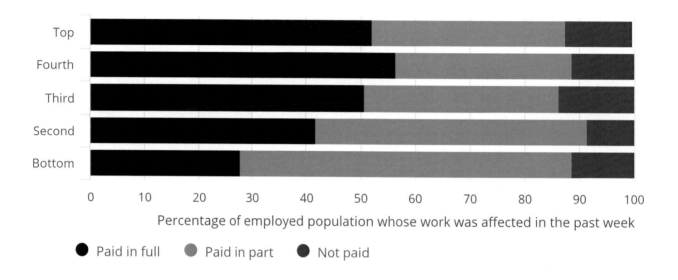

Figure 2: People on higher incomes were more likely to be paid in full if they were unable to work, compared with those on lower incomes

Percentage of people responding to whether they were still being paid while their work was on hold, by income quintile band for financial year ending 2020, Great Britain, May 2020 to October 2020

Source: Office for National Statistics – Survey of Living Conditions

Notes:

1. Responses to the question "Over the past week, are you still being paid whilst your job is on hold/affected by coronavirus (COVID-19)?".

2. Base population: Those people who were employed and stated that they were unable to do any work over the past week.

3. Individuals are ranked by their equivalised household disposable income for financial year ending 2020, using the modified OECD scale.

4. Please see glossary definition of income quintiles.

Of those whose work was affected by the coronavirus at any point in the pandemic, people who were in the bottom quintile of the income distribution (as measured by their income in the same period of the previous year) were much more likely to be paid in part (60.9%) than in full (27.8%). By contrast, over half (52%) of people in the top quintile of the income distribution were paid in full.

Figure 3: Those in the lowest part of the income distribution who were working or unemployed were more likely to report reduced household income

Percentage of economically active population reporting on whether household income has changed, split by income quintile band for financial year ending 2020, Great Britain, April 2020 to October 2020

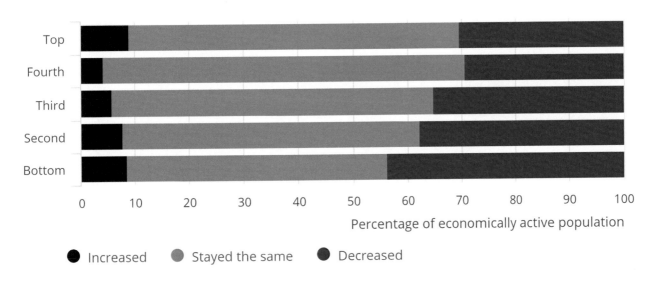

Figure 3: Those in the lowest part of the income distribution who were working or unemployed were more likely to report reduced household income

Percentage of economically active population reporting on whether household income has changed, split by income quintile band for financial year ending 2020, Great Britain, April 2020 to October 2020

Source: Office for National Statistics – Survey of Living Conditions

Notes:

1. Responses to the question "Has your household income changed at all since the start of the coronavirus outbreak in the UK?".

2. Individuals are ranked by their equivalised household disposable income for financial year ending 2020, using the modified OECD scale.

3. Please see glossary definition of income quintiles

For those working or unemployed (classed as economically active), those in poorer households were more likely to report reduced income, as well as being more likely to be furloughed and paid in part if this were to occur. The proportion of economically active people who reported reduced income was 43.8% among those in the lowest income quintile, which compares with only 30.4% of those in the top income quintile.

However, in the economically inactive population, the proportion of people reporting reduced income was much smaller at approximately 13% across all income quintiles. This group tends to receive most of their income from pensions, property income (for example, rental income) or benefits, and are therefore less likely to be impacted by disruptions to the labour market. Even when constrained to people of working age, the proportion reporting reduced income was equal across the quintiles.

There were substantial differences across age groups in the proportion of employed people reporting lower income. Among those aged 16 to 30 years, 12.3% with a job reported reduced income over the period 16 to 20 December 2020, with the figure much higher for those aged 30 to 59 years at 17.9%, while only 6.5% of those aged over 60 years reported this. These differences across age groups have remained stable since the pandemic began.

Figure 4: Comparing the end of 2020 with the first lockdown, fewer employed parents reported reduced income

Share of the employed population reporting a reduced household income, split by parental status, Great Britain, 3 April 2020 to 20 December 2020

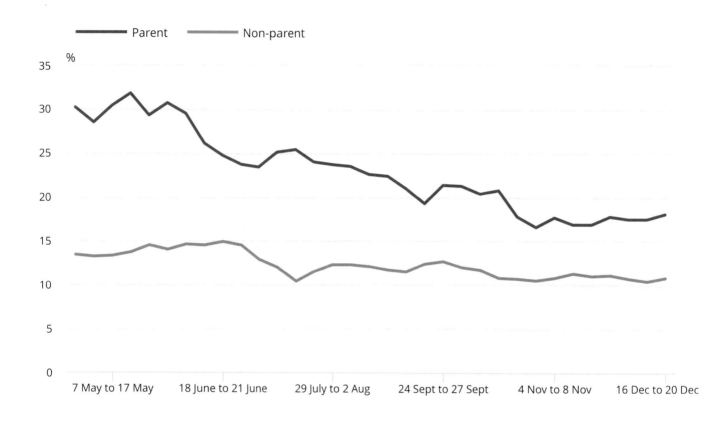

Source: Office for National Statistics – Opinions and Lifestyle Survey

Notes:

1. Responses to the question "In the past seven days, how have your household finances been affected?".

2. Share of respondents who responded "I have reduced income".

3. Four-period rolling average has been calculated.

4. See glossary definition of parents.

In addition, a greater proportion of employed parents with children in the home also reported reduced income throughout 2020. At the start of the pandemic, parents in work were more than twice as likely to report reduced income than non-parents in work (31.7% and 15.1% respectively). This decreased over the course of the pandemic, with only 17.1% of parents reporting reduced income in the five days to 20 December 2020, compared with 12% of non-parents reporting this over the same period.

Self-employed people were more likely to report reduced hours and income compared with the employee population. In December 2020, the self-employed were around 5.5 times more likely to report reduced hours than employees, up from the first lockdown where they were between two and four times more likely.

Almost one-quarter (24.2%) of self-employed people had received support from the Self-Employment Income Support Scheme (SEISS) up to October 2020. In comparison, 17.6% of employees were receiving or had at some point received support from the Coronavirus Job Retention Scheme (CJRS).

Figure 5: Those accessing the Self-employment Income Support Scheme were more likely to report reduced income compared with those on the employee job retention scheme

Share of employees and self-employed who reported that their household income had decreased or stayed the same, and whether they received support from the SEISS or CJRS, Great Britain, May 2020 to October 2020

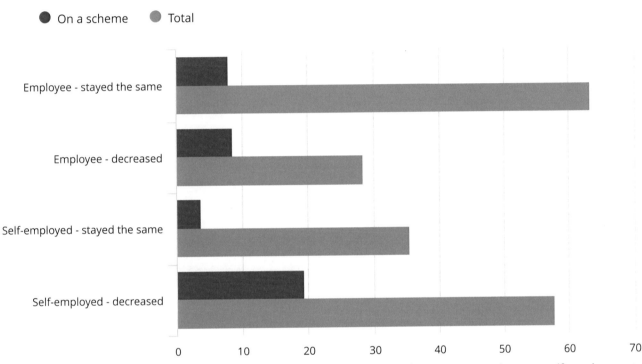

Percentage of economically active who stated that their main job was as an employee or self-employment

Source: Office for National Statistics – Survey of Living Conditions

Notes:

1. Responses to the questions "Has your household income changed at all since the start of the coronavirus outbreak in the UK?" and "Are you at present receiving (or have you received at any point) support from any of the following schemes?".

2. People on a scheme refers to people on CJRS for employees and people on SEISS for the self-employed.

3. Base population: Those people who were economically active and stated that their main job was as an employee or self-employment.

The self-employed accessing the SEISS were more likely to report reduced income compared with those on the CJRS. This may be a result of employers having the ability to "top-up" wages above the government's contribution, while SEISS payments were based on a proportion of average historical trading profit.

3 . Savings, borrowing and affordability

Over the course of 2020, there was an increase in the number of people borrowing more money, and in larger amounts. This coincided with a decrease in people being able to save for the year ahead, with lower income groups, self-employed and people who rent accommodation most affected.

Figure 6: By December 2020, nearly 9 million people had to borrow more money than usual, with the proportion borrowing £1,000 or more increasing since June 2020

Number of people reporting that they had to borrow more because of the coronavirus, and share of those borrowing under and over £1,000, Great Britain, 25 June 2020 to 6 December 2020

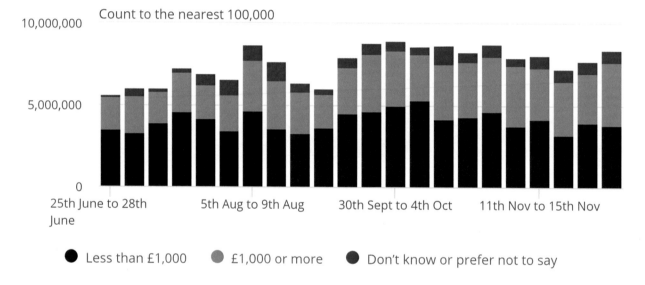

Figure 6: By December 2020, nearly 9 million people had to borrow more money than usual, with the proportion borrowing £1,000 or more increasing since June 2020

Number of people reporting that they had to borrow more because of the coronavirus, and share of those borrowing under and over £1,000, Great Britain, 25 June 2020 to 6 December 2020

Source: Office for National Statistics – Opinions and Lifestyle Survey

Notes:

1. Responses to the question "Have you had to borrow more money or use more credit than usual since the coronavirus outbreak? (Borrowing or using credit includes credit cards, overdrafts, or taking out loans, borrowing from friends, family, neighbours or other personal connections.)" and "How much more money have you borrowed or spent using credit since the coronavirus (COVID-19) outbreak?".

2. Share of respondents who responded "Less than £1,000", "More than £1,000", "Don't know" and "Don't know/Prefer not to say".

At the end of June 2020, 10.8% of adults reported borrowing money, rising to 17.4% in December 2020. Of those, the proportion borrowing more than £1,000 increased from 34.7% to 45.1% in the same period.

Self-employed people were more likely to borrow more than £1,000 than employees in early December 2020 (60.9% versus 49.4% of those who borrowed), and there was a large increase in the proportion of disabled individuals borrowing more than £1,000 (rising from 12.8% to 36.2% of all that borrowed since June).

As the pandemic progressed, increasing proportions of people reported that they would not be able to save for the year ahead. At the end of March 2020, 31.6% of people said they would be unable to save, increasing to 38.4% in mid-December 2020.

Groups that found it harder to save included those on incomes below £20,000, self-employed individuals and people living in rented accommodation (Table 1). Conversely, the under-30 age group consistently reported being more likely to be able to save than other age groups.

Table 1: Fewer people were able to save for the year ahead, and some groups were disproportionately affected
Proportion of people reporting that they would be able to save for the year ahead, Great Britain, March 2020 to December 2020

Groups	Beginning of pandemic	December	Average over the period
Total population	40.6%	41.2%	38.2%
Household income below £20,000	37.9%	30.4%	30.3%
Household income above £20,000	51.2%	60.1%	53.1%
Self-employed	24.3%	28.5%	29.8%
Employees	44.8%	49.3%	44.8%
Living in rented accommodation	34.7%	30.1%	25.5%
Homeowner with a mortgage	44.2%	48.9%	43.6%
Homeowner (owned outright)	42.6%	44.4%	42.1%
Under 30 age group	57.5%	45.5%	38.5%
30-59 age group	36.6%	40.6%	35.9%
60 and over age group	35.8%	39.4%	35.4%

Source: Office for National Statistics – Opinions and Lifestyle Survey

Notes

1. Responses answering "Yes" to the question "In view of the general economic situation, do you think you will be able to save any money in the next twelve months?".

2. Other options were "No" and "Prefer not to say".

3. The "Beginning of the Pandemic" refers to the period 27 March 2020 to 6 April 2020, "December" refers to the period 16 to 20 December 2020.

4. Household incomes below £20,000 were calculated as a simple average of those in household incomes up to £10,000, and between £10,000 and £20,000, and similarly for those above £20,000, it is a simple average of those between £20,000 to £40,000 and those above that amount.

5. Average over the period is calculated as a simple average from 27 March to 20 December 2020.

Despite the need to borrow more and save less, the proportion of individuals who were unable to afford an unexpected but necessary expense of £850 remained stable throughout the pandemic period, with a weekly average of 31% from 9 April to 20 December 2020.

However, some groups found it easier to afford an unexpected expense than others. From April to October 2020, individuals aged under 30 years were less likely to report being able to afford an unexpected expense (62.9%) than individuals aged 30 to 59 years (72.5%) or those aged 60 years and over (84%). Similarly, parents were less able to afford an unexpected expense (64.3%) than non-parents (79.7%).

These differences could also be observed when respondents were asked if their household could afford a week's annual holiday away from home, with younger individuals and parents (70.2% and 71.8% respectively) less able to afford a holiday than older individuals and non-parents (85.4% and 82.1% respectively).

The ease with which individuals have been able to pay their usual expenses has also differed over the course of the pandemic. From April to October 2020, 27.3% of people had some degree of difficulty paying their usual expenses.

The most influenced groups of the population included individuals aged under 30 years who were more likely to report having difficulty meeting their expenses (34%) compared with those aged 30 to 59 years (26.5%) or aged 60 years and over (18.8%). Parents were also more likely to have difficulty meeting their expenses (33.7%) than non-parents (20.6%).

4 . Personal well-being and expectations for the future

Since the initial lockdown at the end of March 2020, levels of both anxiety and happiness have seen substantial and significant improvement. Looking at the week ending 30 March, the mean rating for anxiety was 5.18 out of 10. By the period of 7 to 11 October this had fallen by 30.5% to 3.97. The improvement in happiness was smaller but still significant, with the mean average increasing by 8.9% from 6.36 in the week ending 30 March to 6.98 in the same period of 7 to 11 October. Expectations about when life would return to normal fluctuated as the pandemic progressed, with more people hopeful that life would return to normal sooner rather than later at the end of the year, and more people increasingly optimistic about their own household finances.

Despite the improvement to levels of happiness and anxiety, they remain significantly worsened compared with pre-pandemic levels. Similarly, mean ratings of life satisfaction and feeling that things done in life are worthwhile remain subdued, particularly for those who reported feeling lonely always or often. For this group, the mean rating of life satisfaction was 3.83 out of 10 in the period of 16 to 20 December 2020, which was 46.5% lower than the overall UK average of 7.16 for the same period.

Previous analysis identified that in the early stages of lockdown, anxiety was significantly higher for women than it was for men. However, in the subsequent weeks, the gap between the sexes narrowed, such that by the week ending 10 May, the gap was no longer significant. For context, prior to lockdown, anxiety was usually higher for women than men. While men and women reported similar levels of life satisfaction early in the pandemic, in the period of 28 October to 1 November, women reported significantly lower life satisfaction than men. The mean rating of 6.34 for women was 5.8% lower than the mean of 6.71 for men. Average levels of personal well-being across different demographic groups are shown in our associated datasets.

On 4 February 2021, quarterly estimates of personal well-being will be published using data from the Annual Population Survey (APS). There will be an article published on the same day that considers the impact that the pandemic has had on data collection, to what extent this has influenced estimates of personal well-being and reviews the comparability between estimates from the OPN and the APS.

In terms of future expectations, fewer people thought that life would either never return to normal, or would take more than a year to do so, from 44.4% of the population for the five days to 25 October 2020 to 26.7% for 16 to 20 December 2020.

Although most people continue to believe that the general economic situation will get worse, this proportion has also fallen, from 85.3% at the start of November 2020 to 68.4% in early December 2020. In addition, people are becoming more optimistic when asked on the prospects for their personal household financial situation. The number of people who expect the financial position of their household to get better over the next 12 months increased from 11.0% in April 2020 to 21.5% at the end of December 2020.

Optimism levels were different depending on an individuals' employment status and age group. For example, self-employed people were 37.5% more likely to expect their household financial situation to get worse, compared with employees, throughout the pandemic. Despite being more likely to have been furloughed recently, those aged under 30 years were the least likely to expect their household finances to get worse throughout the pandemic.

Figure 7: People's perspectives on their personal household financial situation have improved slightly since summer

Proportion of respondents who thought their personal household financial situation would get better, stay the same or get worse, Great Britain, 27 March 2020 to 6 December 2020

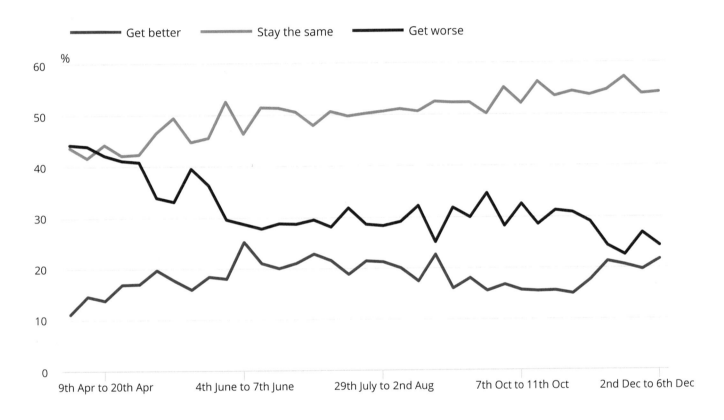

Notes:

Source: Office for National Statistics – Opinions and Lifestyle Survey

1. Responses to the question: "How do you expect the financial position of your household to change over the next 12 months?".

2. Share of respondents who responded: "Get Better", "Stay the Same" and "Get Worse".

5 . Personal and economic well-being data

Total population estimates on personal and economic well-being across time
Dataset | 21 January 2021
Total population estimates on personal and economic well-being across time according to the Opinions and Lifestyle Survey.

Economic well-being estimates from the Survey of Living Conditions, Great Britain
Dataset | 21 January 2021
Estimates of how the coronavirus (COVID-19) has impacted income and affordability in Great Britain. Data are from the Survey of Living Conditions (SLC).

Income group split estimates on personal and economic well-being across time
Dataset | 25 January 2021
Income group split estimates on personal and economic well-being across time according to the Opinions and Lifestyle Survey.

Parental split estimates on personal and economic well-being across time
Dataset | 25 January 2021
Parental split estimates on personal and economic well-being across time according to the Opinions and Lifestyle Survey.

Age group split estimates on personal and economic well-being across time
Dataset | 25 January 2021
Age group split estimates on personal and economic well-being across time according to the Opinions and Lifestyle Survey.

6 . Glossary

Coronavirus Job Retention Scheme (CJRS)

The Coronavirus Job Retention Scheme, also known as the furlough scheme, provides support to employees by providing 80% of their current salary for hours that they are unable to work because of the coronavirus (COVID-19).

Economic activity

The economically active includes those who are unemployed and employed (including furloughed workers, those on maternity or paternity leave and annual or sick leave). Unemployment measures people without a job who have been actively seeking work within the last four weeks and are available to start work within the next two weeks.

The economically inactive refers to people who are not in the labour force as they have not been seeking work within the last four weeks and/or they are unable to start work in the next two weeks.

Economic well-being

Our economic well-being measures present a rounded and comprehensive basis for assessing changes in economic well-being through indicators that adjust or supplement more traditional measures such as gross domestic product (GDP).

Income quintiles

Individuals are ranked by their equivalised household disposable incomes, using the modified Organisation for Economic Co-operation and Development (OECD) scale, and then divided into five income quintiles.

Self-Employment Income Support Scheme (SEISS)

The government introduced the Coronavirus (COVID-19) Self-Employment Income Support Scheme to support self-employed people affected by the economic impact of the coronavirus. This was a taxable grant worth 80% of trading profits up to a maximum of £2,500 per month for three months from March 2020. Self-employed workers were then able to make a claim for a second and final grant in August 2020.

Parent

In this publication, a respondent is classified as a parent if they live with a dependent child aged under 16 years.

Personal well-being

Our personal well-being measures ask people to evaluate, on a scale of 0 to 10, how satisfied they are with their life overall, whether they feel they have meaning and purpose in their life, and about their emotions (happiness and anxiety) during a particular period.

Income

Respondents are asked about their personal income and grouped into bands accordingly. This is the total annual income for that individual from all sources, gross of tax.

Respondents are also asked about the effects of the coronavirus (COVID-19) pandemic on their household income. This is the total annual income from all sources for all individuals in the same household.

7 . Measuring the data

Data sources

The statistics in this publication are based on the Office for National Statistics' (ONS's) weekly Opinions and Lifestyle Survey (OPN), which was created to understand the impact of the coronavirus (COVID-19) pandemic on British society and the Survey on Living Conditions (SLC), which is the longitudinal component of the Household Finances Survey (HFS).

The data analysed mostly cover the period 20 March to 20 December 2020 and consider the impact on measures of personal and economic well-being during the whole period, from initial lockdown and restrictions through to easing over summer and the reintroduction of restrictions from September 2020 onwards. High-level analysis beyond 20 December 2020 can be found in our weekly release on Coronavirus and the social impacts on Great Britain.

Opinions and Lifestyle Survey (OPN)

The OPN is a monthly omnibus survey. In response to the coronavirus pandemic, we have adapted the OPN to become a weekly survey used to collect data on the impact of the coronavirus pandemic on day-to-day life in Great Britain. Throughout the bulletin, analysis using the weekly module from the OPN is used. For the time periods covered in each module, please see our reference tables. In the latest wave, 6,027 individuals were sampled, with a response rate of 55.3% (or 3,300 individuals) for the survey conducted from 16 to 20 December 2020.

The survey results are weighted to be a nationally representative sample for Great Britain, and data are collected using an online self-completion questionnaire. Individuals who did not want to or were unable to complete the survey online had the opportunity to take part over the phone.

Sampling

A sample of 6,027 households was randomly selected from those that had previously completed the Labour Market Survey (LMS). From each household, one adult was selected at random but with unequal probability. Younger people were given higher selection probability than other people because of under-representation in the sample available for the survey. The survey also includes a boosted sample for England to allow more detailed analysis at a regional level, which are available in the datasets.

Weighting

The responding sample in the week 22 December 2020 to 3 January 2021 contained 3,756 individuals (62% response rate). Survey weights were applied to make estimates representative of the population.

Weights were first adjusted for non-response and attrition. Subsequently, the weights were calibrated to satisfy population distributions considering the following factors:

- sex by age

- region

- tenure

- highest qualification

- employment status

For age, sex and region, population totals based on projections of mid-year population estimates for December 2020 were used. The resulting weighted sample is therefore representative of the Great Britain adult population by a number of socio-demographic factors and geography.

Survey of Living Conditions (SLC)

The SLC is a six-year, wave survey that serves as the longitudinal component of the Household Finances Survey (HFS), used in the ONS's annual releases into average household income. This analysis is based on 13,635 responses from individuals collected between April and October 2020, which have been linked with data from the previous wave of data collection (April to October 2019) where available.

As such, the SLC provides the possibility of longitudinal analysis, looking at how the situation has changed from one year to the next for a cohort of households. This is particularly useful for looking at household's finances before and during the coronavirus pandemic.

Sampling

The sample is produced by randomly selecting 1,340 postcode sectors in Great Britain and then splitting these into eight equal bands based on socio-economic classification and ordering according to car ownership, before randomly selecting 15 households from each postcode sector. It captures roughly 2,500 unique variables on topics including housing, employment, health and income.

Additionally, since the start of the coronavirus pandemic, variables have been added to explore how people's lives and particularly household finances have been affected by COVID-19.

Weighting

Survey weights were applied to make estimates representative of the population. Weights were not adjusted for non-response and attrition to provide more timely estimates, but weights were calibrated to satisfy population distributions considering the following factors: sex by age, region and tenure. Tenure has recently been added to the survey weightings to address changing demographics of respondents (see Strengths and limitations).

8 . Strengths and limitations

Opinions and Lifestyle Survey (OPN)

The main strengths of the Opinions and Lifestyle Survey (OPN) include:

- it allows for timely production of data and statistics that can respond quickly to changing needs

- it meets data needs: the questionnaire is developed with customer consultation, and design expertise is applied in the development stages

- robust methods are adopted for the survey's sampling and weighting strategies to limit the impact of bias

- quality assurance procedures are undertaken throughout the analysis stages to minimise the risk of error

The main limitations of the OPN include:

- analysis of estimates in Wales and Scotland are based on low sample sizes, and therefore caution should be used with these estimates

- comparisons between periods and groups must be done with caution as estimates are provided from a sample survey; as such, confidence intervals are included in the datasets to present the sampling variability, which should be taken into account when assessing differences between periods, as true differences may not exist

Survey of Living Conditions (SLC)

The main strength of the Survey of Living Conditions (SLC) is its use as a dedicated survey into household income and earnings. Because of the longitudinal nature, respondents are used to providing a wealth of financial data that allow for the creation of detailed estimates of household income. This also allows for comparison across multiple years to see how a household's income has changed over time.

Analysis using the SLC is experimental with early indicators derived from simple frequency counts of variables included in the questionnaire. The aim of this is to provide timely data that reflect the changing picture of household income throughout the COVID-19 pandemic. The analysis has been produced before any imputation is carried out.

Imputation is crucial to the estimation of income measures, therefore, at present, measures of income are not provided. The questions best suited to be used as early indicators are "opinion" questions or those relating to "reported changes" (increase, decrease or stayed the same) in income, and so this has been the focus of the analysis provided.

As with all survey-based sources, the data are subject to some limitations. For instance, the SLC is a sample of the private household population, and therefore does not include those that live in institutionalised households, such as care homes and hostels, or the homeless. As such, it is likely that many of the poorest in society are not captured, which users should bear in mind when interpreting these statistics.

In response to the coronavirus pandemic, the SLC has been adapted from being collected face-to-face, using computer-assisted questionnaires, to telephone collection. This has affected the sample that has responded to the survey, which seems to have become biased towards people who own their home. To address this, the weightings have been adjusted to include tenure.

9 . Related links

Household income inequality, UK: financial year ending 2020
Bulletin | Released 21 January 2021
Provisional estimates of income inequality in the UK for the financial year ending 2020.

Average household income, UK: financial year ending 2020 (provisional)
Bulletin | Released 21 January 2021
Provisional estimates of median and mean disposable income for people in the UK for the financial year ending 2020.

Personal well-being in the UK: April 2019 to March 2020
Bulletin | Released 30 July 2020
Estimates of life satisfaction, feeling that the things done in life are worthwhile, happiness and anxiety at the UK, country, regional, county and local authority level. Covering the period in the build up to the national lockdown of the UK in response to the coronavirus (COVID-19) pandemic.

Coronavirus and anxiety, Great Britain: 3 April 2020 to 10 May 2020
Article | Released 15 June 2020
The number of people reporting high levels of anxiety has sharply elevated during the coronavirus (COVID-19) pandemic. This article will provide insights into which socio-demographic and economic factors were most associated with high levels of anxiety during the first weeks of lockdown.

Coronavirus and the social impacts on Great Britain: 15 January 2021
Bulletin | Released 15 January 2021
Indicators from the Opinions and Lifestyle Survey covering the period 7 to 10 January 2021 to understand the impact of the coronavirus (COVID-19) pandemic on people, households and communities in Great Britain.

Office for
National Statistics

Statistical bulletin

Personal and economic well-being in Great Britain: May 2021

Estimates from multiple sources for personal and economic well-being to understand the economic impact of the coronavirus (COVID-19) pandemic on households in Great Britain from March 2020 to April 2021.

Contact:
Bella Beynon and Gueorguie Vassilev
PeopleAndProsperity@ons.gov.uk
+44 (0)1633455330 or +44 (0) 1633 456265

Release date:
25 May 2021

Next release:
To be announced

Notice

25 May 2021

Previous data tables released in January 2021 contained small errors in the data and some inconsistencies in secondary suppression. This did not affect any of the findings in the previous article. Please use the new data tables which cover the whole period. We apologise for any inconvenience caused.

Table of contents

1 . Main points

- Those groups that were financially impacted at the start of the coronavirus (COVID-19) pandemic were still worse off up to mid-April 2021; such as the self-employed, who were three times as likely to report reduced income and twice as likely to use savings to cover living costs compared with employees.

- Those in the lowest income bracket (up to £10,000 per annum) continued to be more likely to report negative impacts to personal well-being in comparison with higher brackets; such as the coronavirus pandemic making their mental health worse (18%) and feeling stressed or anxious (32%).

- Those in the highest income brackets (£40,000 a year or more) continued to be more likely to report that the coronavirus pandemic was negatively impacting their working life, and were six times as likely to report the pandemic was having a strain on their working relationships; those employed were over twice as likely to find working from home difficult than those in the lowest income bracket.

- Employed parents were less likely to be furloughed since the beginning of 2021, unlike in the first phase of lockdown, but were still more likely to report reduced income than non-parents; despite the financial impacts, all parents continued to feel less lonely and report higher scores of feeling that things done in life are worthwhile.

- Those aged under 30 years were consistently more likely to report that their income had been reduced (15%) than those over 60 years (5%); however, a higher proportion of those under 30 years reported being able to save for the year ahead (50%) than older age groups (39%).

- Perceptions of incomes and savings also appeared to differ; for example, those in the youngest age group were less financially resilient than older age groups, with 47% of those under 30 years reporting that they could afford an unexpected expense compared with 71% of those over 60 years, despite a higher proportion reporting that they were able to save for the year ahead.

2 . Statistician's comment

"The initial pandemic shock saw millions of individuals suffer both financially and with their well-being. This continues to be felt more than a year on, with similar amounts of people needing to borrow or use savings to make ends meet as seen last year. Worryingly, the self-employed, parents, young people and those living on the lowest household incomes remain more negatively affected by the pandemic in April 2021."

Gueorguie Vassilev, Head of Economic Well-being.

3 . Personal and economic well-being data

Total population estimates on personal and economic well-being across time
Dataset | 25 May 2021
Total population estimates on personal and economic well-being across time according to the Opinions and Lifestyle Survey.

Economic well-being estimates from the Survey of Living Conditions, Great Britain
Dataset | 25 May 2021
Estimates of how the coronavirus (COVID-19) has impacted income and affordability in Great Britain. Data are from the Survey of Living Conditions (SLC).

Income group split estimates on personal and economic well-being across time
Dataset | 25 May 2021-
Income group split estimates on personal and economic well-being across time according to the Opinions and Lifestyle Survey.

Parental split estimates on personal and economic well-being across time
Dataset | 25 May 2021
Parental split estimates on personal and economic well-being across time according to the Opinions and Lifestyle Survey.

Age group split estimates on personal and economic well-being across time
Dataset | 25 May 2021
Age group split estimates on personal and economic well-being across time according to the Opinions and Lifestyle Survey.

4 . Measuring the data

For details on the data sources, sampling and weighting, please see the Measuring the data section in our previous release.

5 . Related links

Personal well-being in the UK, quarterly: April 2011 to September 2020
Bulletin | Released 4 April 2021
Quarterly estimates of life satisfaction, feeling that the things done in life are worthwhile, happiness and anxiety at the UK level, created using the Annual Population Survey (APS).

Household income inequality, UK: financial year ending 2020
Bulletin | Released 21 January 2021
Initial insight into main estimates of household incomes and inequality in the UK, along with analysis of how these measures have changed over time accounting for inflation and household composition.

Average household income, UK: financial year ending 2020
Bulletin | Released 21 January 2021
Final estimates of average household income in the UK, with analysis of how these measures have changed over time, accounting for inflation and household composition.

Coronavirus and anxiety, Great Britain: 3 April 2020 to 10 May 2020
Article | Released 15 June 2020
The number of people reporting high levels of anxiety has sharply elevated during the coronavirus (COVID-19) pandemic. This article will provide insights into which socio-demographic and economic factors were most associated with high levels of anxiety during the first weeks of lockdown.

Coronavirus and the social impacts on Great Britain: 21 May 2021
Bulletin | Released 15 January 2021
Indicators from the Opinions and Lifestyle Survey covering the period 12 to 16 May 2021 to understand the impact of the coronavirus (COVID-19) pandemic on people, households and communities in Great Britain.

Statistical bulletin

Personal well-being in the UK: April 2020 to March 2021

Estimates of life satisfaction, feeling that the things done in life are worthwhile, happiness and anxiety at the UK, country, regional, county and local authority level.

Contact:
Laurence Day
qualityoflife@ons.gov.uk
+44 1633 456300

Release date:
15 October 2021

Next release:
To be announced

Table of contents

1 . Main points

- Average ratings of well-being have deteriorated across all indicators in the year ending March 2021, continuing a trend that was seen across most indicators in the previous period, but even more sharply, and which notably takes place entirely during the coronavirus (COVID-19) pandemic.

- The most recent annual declines in personal well-being in the UK were the greatest we have seen since we started measuring personal well-being for life satisfaction (0.27 point decline), anxiety (0.26 point increase), happiness (0.17 point decline) and feeling that the things done in life are worthwhile (0.15 point decline).

- Average ratings of anxiety increased in all countries and regions of the UK compared with the previous period apart from Northern Ireland and the North East, with the largest increases being in the West Midlands (0.44 point increase) and the North West (0.38 point increase).

- Average ratings of happiness declined in all countries and regions of the UK compared with the previous period apart from the North East and the East Midlands, with the largest decreases being in the West Midlands (0.22 point decrease) and Yorkshire and The Humber (0.20 point decrease).

- Average ratings of life satisfaction declined in all countries and regions of the UK compared with the previous period, with the largest decreases being in Northern Ireland (0.32 point decrease) and Yorkshire and The Humber (0.31 point decrease).

- Average ratings of feeling that the things done in life are worthwhile declined in all countries and regions of the UK apart from the North East, with the largest decrease being in the South East (0.19 point decrease).

Because of small sample sizes and large confidence intervals estimates for local authorities should not be ranked against each other.

2 . Personal well-being data time series

The annual period covered in this release is the first to take place entirely during the coronavirus (COVID-19) pandemic. Figure 1 shows how measures of personal well-being have changed on an annual basis for the UK as a whole from the year ending March 2012 to March 2021. The datasets accompanying the bulletin provide estimates for each local authority in the UK, presenting a picture of well-being in local authorities during the coronavirus pandemic.

This release contains official estimates of personal well-being from 2011 onwards collected by the Annual Population Survey at national and sub-national level. More frequent national level well-being estimates during the coronavirus pandemic are also available from the ONS Opinions Survey. For more on the difference between well-being estimates from the two surveys please read Data collection changes due to the pandemic and their impact on estimating personal well-being.

Figure 1: Personal well-being deteriorated across the year ending March 2021

Average personal well-being ratings, UK, years ending March 2012 to March 2021

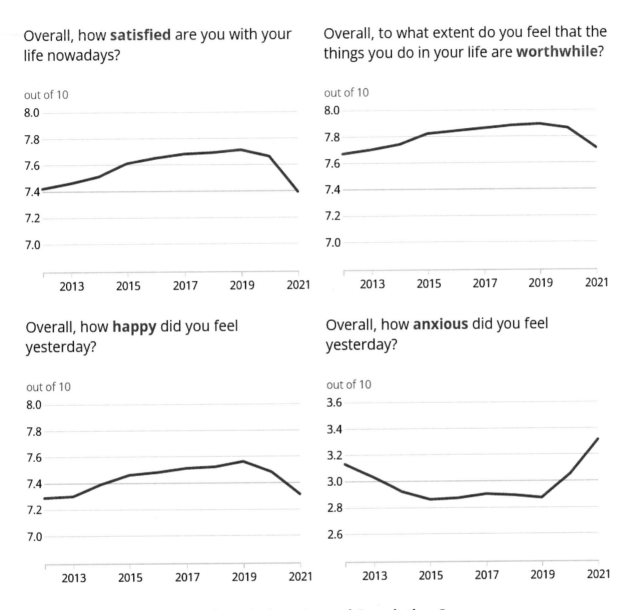

Source: Office for National Statistics – Annual Population Survey

Notes:

1. The y-axis has a break in it, meaning it does not necessarily start from zero.

2. Data are weighted mean averages.

3. The personal well-being measures were first collected in England, Scotland and Wales at local level in April 2011 while in Northern Ireland in April 2012. The first year from which we have a full UK baseline at local level is therefore the year ending March 2013.

4. From 2021 the local authority breakdowns for Northern Ireland derived from the Annual Population Survey no longer represent the official well-being statistics used by the Northern Ireland Statistics and Research Agency, as these have been changed to the Northern Ireland Continuous Household Survey.

3 . Personal well-being by local area

Our personal well-being explorer tools shown in Figures 2 and 3 allow everyone to observe well-being in their local area and compare it with other areas.

Ranking local authorities based on their average scores may be misleading for various reasons such as different sample sizes, different confidence intervals and mode effects, as well as not comparing like with like. Comparisons between areas should be made with caution, and confidence intervals should be taken into account when assessing differences.

Figure 2: Personal well-being interactive maps

Average ratings of personal well-being, UK, years ending March 2012 to March 2021

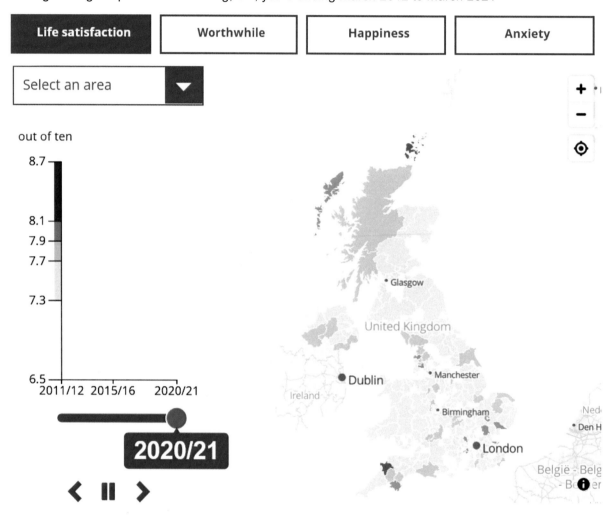

Source: Annual Population Survey, ONS

Note: This is a snapshot of an interactive image, to view the full image please go to: https://www.ons.gov.uk/peoplepopulationandcommunity/wellbeing/bulletins/measuringnationalwellbeing/april2020tomarch2021

Notes:

1. Data are weighted mean averages.

2. The personal well-being measures were first collected in England, Scotland and Wales at local level in April 2011 while in Northern Ireland in April 2012. The first year from which we have a full UK baseline at local level is therefore the year ending March 2013.

3. From 2021 the local authority breakdowns for Northern Ireland derived from the Annual Population Survey no longer represent the official well-being statistics used by the Northern Ireland Statistics and Research Agency, as these have been changed to the Northern Ireland Continuous Household Survey.

4. Rounding processes may differ from those used in the datasets.

Figure 3: Personal well-being explorer

Average ratings of personal well-being, UK, years ending March 2012 to March 2021

| Life satisfaction | Worthwhile | Happiness | Anxiety |

Start typing some areas, or click the lines to select up to six areas

Choose some areas

Out of ten

9

8.5

8

7.5

7

6.5

6

2011/12 2012/13 2013/14 2014/15 2015/16 2016/17 2017/18 2018/19 2019/20 2020/21

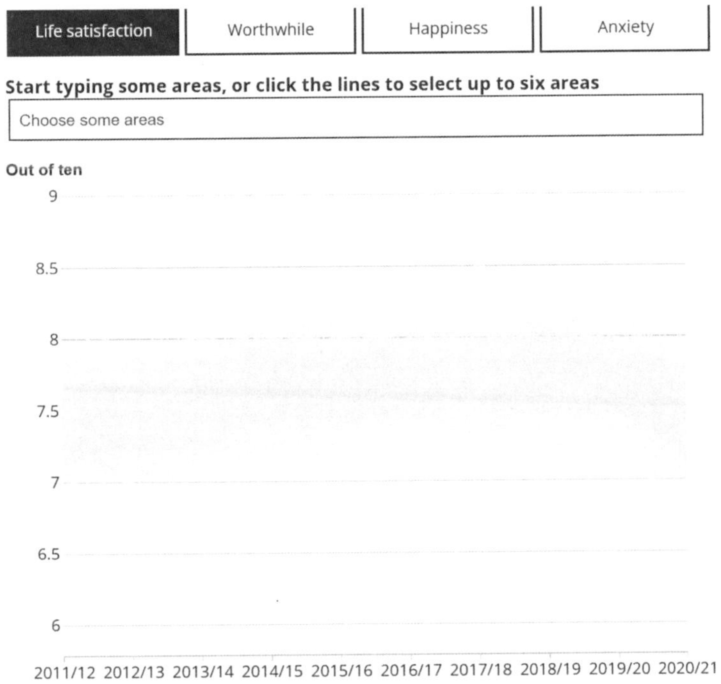

Source: Office for National Statistics - Annual Population Survey

Note: This is a snapshot of an interactive image, to view the full image please go to: https://www.ons.gov.uk/peoplepopulationandcommunity/wellbeing/bulletins/measuringnationalwellbeing/april2020tomarch2021

Average ratings of personal well-being, UK, years ending March 2012 to March 2021

Download the data

Notes:

1. Data are weighted mean averages.

2. The personal well-being measures were first collected in England, Scotland and Wales at local level in April 2011 while in Northern Ireland in April 2012. The first year from which we have a full UK baseline at local level is therefore the year ending March 2013.

3. From 2021 the local authority breakdowns for Northern Ireland derived from the Annual Population Survey no longer represent the official well-being statistics used by the Northern Ireland Statistics and Research Agency, as these have been changed to the Northern Ireland Continuous Household Survey.

4. Rounding processes may differ from those used in the datasets.

4 . Personal well-being data

Annual personal well being estimates
Dataset | Released 15 October 2021
Annual estimates of life satisfaction, feeling that the things done in life are worthwhile, happiness and anxiety in the UK, by local authority and UK and country level.

Quality information for annual personal well-being estimates
Dataset | Released 15 October 2021
Confidence intervals and sample sizes for annual estimates of personal well-being in the UK, by local authority and UK and country level.

5 . Glossary

Personal well-being

Our personal well-being measures ask people to evaluate, on a scale of 0 to 10, how satisfied they are with their life overall, whether they feel they have meaning and purpose in their life, and about their emotions (happiness and anxiety) during a particular period.

Thresholds

Thresholds are used to present dispersion in the data. For the life satisfaction, worthwhile and happiness questions, ratings are grouped in the following way:

- 0 to 4 (low)

- 5 to 6 (medium)

- 7 to 8 (high)

- 9 to 10 (very high)

For the anxiety question, ratings are grouped differently to reflect the fact that higher anxiety is associated with lower personal well-being. The ratings for anxiety are grouped as follows:

- 0 to 1 (very low)

- 2 to 3 (low)

- 4 to 5 (medium)

- 6 to 10 (high)

Mode effects

Testing has shown that people respond more positively to the personal well-being questions when interviewed by telephone rather than face-to-face. As people are interviewed using both methods on the Annual Population Survey, this will have some effect on the personal well-being results.

6 . Measuring the data

Since 2011, we have asked personal well-being questions to adults aged 16 years and over in the UK to better understand how they feel about their lives. This release presents headline results for the year ending March 2021, along with changes over time since we started collecting well-being data in 2011. It provides data at a national level, country and local authority level. The four personal well-being questions are:

- Overall, how satisfied are you with your life nowadays?

- Overall, to what extent do you feel the things you do in your life are worthwhile?

- Overall, how happy did you feel yesterday?

- Overall, how anxious did you feel yesterday?

People are asked to respond on a scale of 0 to 10, where 0 is "not at all" and 10 is "completely". We produce estimates of the mean ratings for all four personal well-being questions, as well as their distributions.

Annual Population Survey (APS)

The annual APS used in this analysis provides the timeliest data on well-being at the granular level by local authority. Further information on the APS can be found on the Annual Population Survey (APS) QMI.

Quality and methodology information covering the elements of the APS related to well-being can be found in the Personal well-being in the UK Quality and Methodology Information report.

There have been some data collection changes to the method used for the Annual Population Survey in response to the coronavirus (COVID-19) pandemic. As a result, the data for this period (April 2020 to March 2021) have a new weighting based on housing tenure. Further information can be found on the following web page: Data collection changes because of the coronavirus (COVID-19) pandemic and their impact on estimating personal well-being.

7 . Strengths and limitations

Accuracy of the statistics: estimating and reporting uncertainty

The personal well-being estimates are from the Annual Population Survey (APS), which provides a representative sample of those living in private residential households in the UK. People living in communal establishments (such as care homes) or other non-household situations are not represented in this survey. This may be important in interpreting the findings in relation to those people reporting lower personal well-being.

As the number of people available in the sample gets smaller, the variability of the estimates that can be made from that sample size gets larger. Estimates for small groups -- for example, respondents from a single local authority (LA) -- which are based on small subsets of the APS, are less reliable and tend to be more volatile than for larger aggregated groups.

From the year ending March 2021, a new set of weights has been used to produce the annual estimates, which are more up to date than the previous weights. Reweighting of the periods prior to the year ending March 2021 will take place at a future date.

From the year ending March 2018, the sample for Northern Ireland received a boost, resulting in greater accuracy in a set of LAs that had had relatively small sample sizes compared with other LAs in the UK.

Statistical significance

Please note that:

- the statistical significance of differences noted within the release are determined based on non-overlapping confidence intervals

- comparisons have been based on unrounded data

8 . Related links

Personal and economic well-being in Great Britain: May 2021
Bulletin | Released on 25 May 2021
Estimates from multiple sources for personal and economic well-being to understand the economic impact of the coronavirus (COVID-19) pandemic on households in Great Britain from March 2020 to April 2021.

Optimism and personal well-being: technical report
Methodology Technical report | Released on 12 March 2020
Exploratory analysis of the relationship between optimism and personal well-being using questions from the 2019 Opinions and Lifestyle (OPN) survey.

Data collection changes due to the pandemic and their impact on estimating personal well-being
Methodology Technical report | Released on 4 February 2021
During the coronavirus (COVID-19) pandemic, the Office for National Statistics has published estimates of personal well-being using both the Annual Population Survey and the weekly module of the Opinions and Lifestyle Survey. This methodology article considers the impact that the pandemic has had on data collection, how this has influenced estimates of personal well-being and the comparability of these estimates.

Coronavirus and the social impacts on Great Britain: 8 October 2021
Dataset | Released on 22 October 2021
Indicators from the Opinions and Lifestyle Survey to understand the impact of the coronavirus (COVID-19) pandemic on people, households and communities in Great Britain.

Measures of national well-being dashboard
Dashboard | Released on 23 October 2019
Latest data, times series data and detailed information for the measures of national well-being.

Coronavirus (COVID-19) latest insights: Well-being
Web portal | Regularly updated

Coronavirus and anxiety, Great Britain: 3 April 2020 to 10 May 2020
Article | Released 15 June 2020
The number of people reporting high levels of anxiety has sharply elevated during the coronavirus (COVID-19) pandemic. This article will provide insights into which socio-demographic and economic factors were most associated with high levels of anxiety during the first weeks of lockdown.

Beyond GDP: How ONS is developing wider measures of well-being
Article | Released 4 February 2019
A summary of how the ONS is continuing to develop new ways of measuring and reporting the UK's economic and social progress and an introduction to the Personal and economic well-being publication.

Statistical bulletin

Personal well-being in the UK, quarterly: April 2011 to June 2021

Quarterly estimates of life satisfaction, feeling that the things done in life are worthwhile, happiness and anxiety in the UK, covering the periods from Quarter 2 (Apr to June) 2011 through to Quarter 2 2021. Age, country and sex sub-population breakdowns of estimates, covering the periods from October 2020 to June 2021, are also included. Estimates were created using the Annual Population Survey (APS).

Contact:
Jackie Massaya
qualityoflife@ons.gov.uk
+44 1633 560 287

Release date:
8 December 2021

Next release:
To be announced

Correction

21 December 2021 12:00

We have corrected an error in section two under the heading "Quarter 1 (Jan to Mar) 2021". The previous version read "respondents with "low" and "high" levels of anxiety declined by 1.4 and 2.0 percentage points, respectively". It should have read "respondents with "medium" and "high" levels of anxiety declined by 1.4 and 2.0 percentage points, respectively". This happened because of a human error.

We have corrected an error in the "download the data" link underneath Figure 1, Figure 2 and Figure 3. The previous version linked data from the previous edition of the "Personal well-being in the UK, quarterly". The "download the data" links should have linked to the data displayed in the charts of Figure 1, Figure 2 and Figure 3.

These happened because of human error. We apologise for any inconvenience caused.

Notice

8 December 2021

Publication of the "Personal well-being in the UK, quarterly" release was suspended due to the coronavirus (COVID-19) pandemic. This release covers the interim three quarters: Quarter 4 (Oct to Dec) 2020, Quarter 1 (Jan to Mar) 2021 and Quarter 2 (Apr to June) 2021.

Table of contents

1 . Main points

- Personal well-being in the UK during the first and second wave of the coronavirus (COVID-19) pandemic is among the lowest levels since we started collecting data in 2011; by the end of the second wave in Quarter 2 (Apr to June) 2021, ratings for feeling that things done in life are worthwhile, happiness and anxiety recovered to levels seen before the coronavirus pandemic in Quarter 4 (Oct to Dec) 2019.

- Soon after the start of the second wave, Quarter 4 2020, average ratings for happiness at the UK level fell to among the lowest scores in a decade (7.23 out of 10); anxiety rose to 3.43 out of 10, which was similar to the highest score recorded at the start of the coronavirus pandemic in Quarter 2 2020

- In Quarter 1 (Jan to Mar) 2021, anxiety fell by 0.20 points to 3.23 at the UK level; the decrease in anxiety was notable for people aged between 50 to 59 and 65 to 74 years, perhaps indicating a sense of optimism as vaccines continued to roll out.

- Improvements in life satisfaction, happiness or anxiety were observed for most age groups by Quarter 2 2021, except for young people (16 to 24 years), those aged between 35 and 39 years and those aged over 84 years.

2 . Personal well-being data over time

This release reports personal well-being on a quarterly basis in the UK from April 2011 to June 2021. The datasets accompanying this bulletin include unadjusted and seasonally-adjusted data at the UK level. Unadjusted estimates for 16 age bands (16 to 19 years through to those aged 90 years or over), the four nations of the UK and both sexes are also provided. This release provides the long-term picture of well-being using the Annual Population Survey (APS). For shorter-term, more timely estimates see results of the ONS Opinions Survey (OPN).

Figure 1: All measures of personal well-being in the UK had largely recovered in Quarter 2 (Apr to June) 2021, from Quarter 4 (Oct to Dec) 2020

Average (mean) ratings of personal well-being in the UK, April 2011 to June 2021

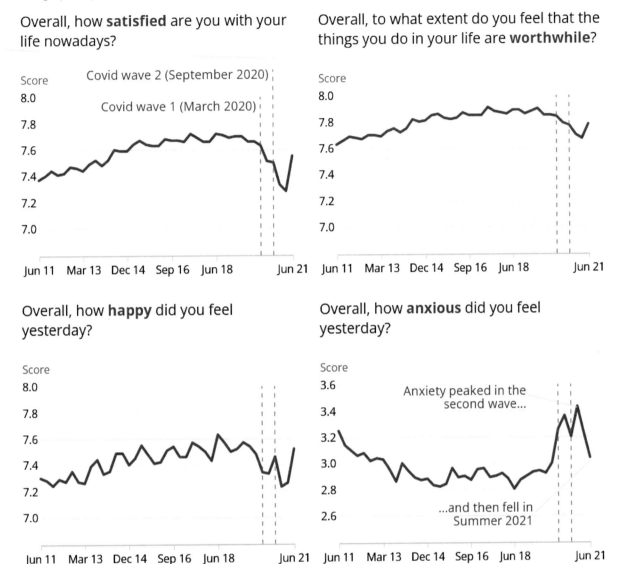

Source: Office for National Statistics – Annual Population Survey

Notes:

1. The y-axis has a break in it, meaning it does not start from zero.

2. Data are non-seasonally adjusted weighted mean averages on a scale of 0 to 10.

Quarter 4 (Oct to Dec) 2020

All personal well-being measures continued to worsen in Quarter 4 (Oct to Dec) 2020. Ratings of happiness and anxiety were the most impacted. Both happiness and anxiety deteriorated by 0.23 points from the previous quarter, from 7.46 to 7.23 out of 10 and from 3.20 to 3.43 out of 10, respectively. Quarter 4 2020 saw ratings of happiness fall to among the lowest scores recorded for a decade, while anxiety ratings were similar to those seen at the start of the coronavirus (COVID-19) pandemic in Quarter 2 (Apr to Jun) 2020. Levels of anxiety during the coronavirus pandemic are the highest since we started collecting well-being data in 2011.

Changes in happiness were driven by a 5.2 percentage point decrease in the proportion of people reporting "very high" happiness levels (32.4% to 27.2% of respondents). During the same period, those reporting "very low" levels of anxiety fell by 4.0 percentage points (34.7% to 30.7% of respondents). Figure 2 shows the changes in thresholds for each well-being measure in each quarter during the period of March 2019 to June 2021

41

Figure 2: The proportion of people reporting "very high" levels of personal well-being increased across October 2020 to June 2021 in the UK

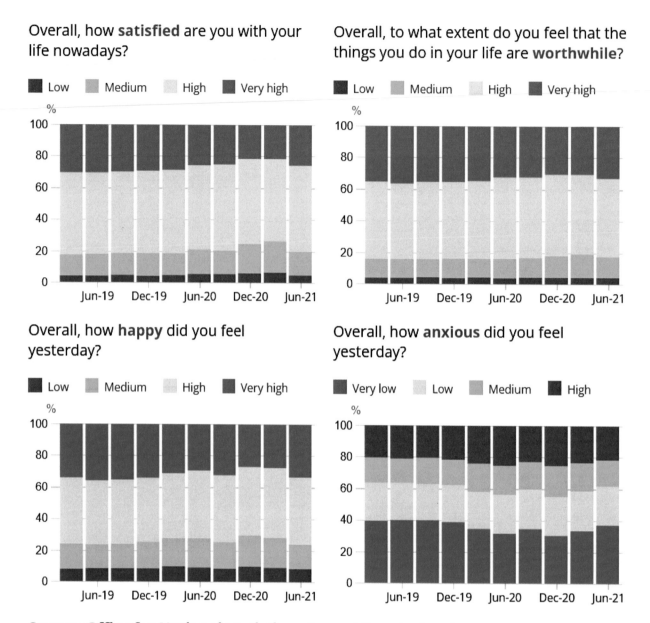

Source: Office for National Statistics – Annual Population Survey

Notes:

1. Please see the glossary for information on the threshold grouping of ratings.

2. Data are non-seasonally adjusted.

Quarter 1 (Jan to Mar) 2021

By Quarter 1 (Jan to Mar) 2021, anxiety fell by 0.20 points to 3.23. Those reporting "very low" anxiety rose by 2.9 percentage points, while respondents with "medium" and "high" levels of anxiety declined by 1.4 and 2.0 percentage points, respectively. These changes are observed within the context of positive developments in the coronavirus response. Vaccines were rolling out at pace and roadmaps to the end of lockdown were announced.

Quarter 2 (Apr to June) 2021

In Quarter 2 (Apr to June) 2021, a "bounce-back" from the downturn of Quarter 4 2020 was seen in all personal well-being measures. Life satisfaction, feeling that the things done in life are worthwhile, and happiness all increased (by 0.27 points to 7.55, 0.11 points to 7.78 and by 0.26 points to 7.52, respectively). Anxiety continued to steeply decline, falling by 0.19 points to 3.04. During this period, lockdown restrictions continued to ease, while the vaccine programme accelerated to being available to all adults in the UK by June 2021.

The percentage of people reporting "very high" levels of life satisfaction, feeling that the things done in life are worthwhile, and happiness all increased by 4.3, 2.2 and 6.1 percentage points, respectively. The number of respondents with "very low" levels of anxiety rose by 3.6 percentage points. These changes drove the improvements in well-being measures from the previous quarter.

People aged 20 to 24 years did not "bounce back" from the high levels of anxiety seen in October to December 2020

By Quarter 2 2021, when on average the UK was experiencing pre-coronavirus pandemic levels of well-being, anxiety in 20- to 24-year-old respondents was significantly higher than the national average (score of 3.56 compared to 3.04 out of 10, respectively). This is a change from the characteristic trend of anxiety over a lifetime. Anxiety tends to peak in middle years (45 to 59 years).

Previous analysis has linked anxiety with loneliness, and young people aged between 16 and 24 years were more likely to experience "lockdown loneliness" during the early stages of the coronavirus pandemic. Over the period covered by Quarter 4 2020 and Quarter 1 2021, higher rates of loneliness were reported in areas with a high population of young people and those who were unemployed. Employment rates of young people aged 16 to 24 years have been the most affected by the coronavirus pandemic, with levels seen in Quarter 2 2021 (51.7%) still below those recorded a year earlier or before the coronavirus pandemic.

In the population aged under 40 years, people aged 25 to 29 years saw the greatest improvement in well-being from October 2020 to June 2021

At the UK level, Quarter 2 2021 saw average life satisfaction return to levels seen at the start of the coronavirus pandemic in Quarter 2 2020. Scores for feeling that things done in life are worthwhile, happiness and anxiety returned to levels last seen before the coronavirus pandemic in Quarter 4 2019.

During the period from Quarter 4 2020 to Quarter 2 2021, improvements in personal well-being for the younger population (those aged under 40 years) were greatest for those aged 25 to 29 years. Life satisfaction of those aged 25 to 29 years rose by 0.34 points (from 7.36 to 7.70), ratings for happiness rose by 0.46 points (from 7.12 to 7.58) and anxiety fell by 0.68 points (from 3.62 to 2.94).

People aged between 16 and 24 years and 35 to 39 years did not report any improvements to any of the personal well-being measures between Quarter 4 2020 and Quarter 2 2021. Those aged 30 to 34 years only reported improvements in life satisfaction, which rose from 7.42 to 7.69.

As a group above the compulsory educational age and below that of the average national age at birth, it is possible that people aged 25 to 29 years are less likely to have been impacted by changes to education and care arrangements for young children during the coronavirus pandemic.

Figure 3: Improving life satisfaction, happiness and anxiety of people aged 25 to 29 years in the UK, over the period Quarter 4 (Oct to Dec) 2020 to Quarter 2 (Apr to June) 2021

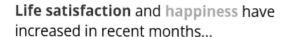

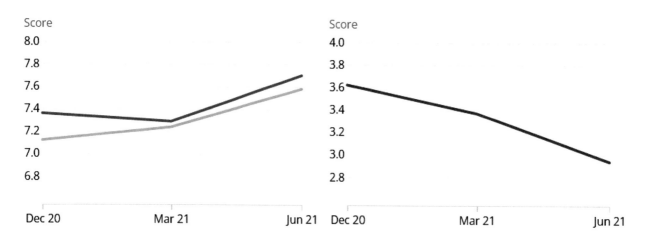

Source: Office for National Statistics – Annual Population Survey

Notes:

1. The y-axis has a break in it, meaning it does not start from zero.

2. Data are non-seasonally adjusted weighted mean averages on a scale of 0 to 10.

People aged 50 to 59 and 65 to 74 years saw a notable fall in anxiety from January to March 2021

In Quarter 1 2021, anxiety fell considerably for people aged 50 to 59 years and 65 to 74 years. This coincides with the progress of the vaccination programme. By the end of March, 77% of those aged 50 to 54, 83% of those aged 55 to 59, 90% of people aged 65 to 69 years and 93% of those aged 70 to 74 years in England had received their first coronavirus vaccine in the first phase of the vaccine roll out.

3 . Personal well-being data

Quarterly personal well-being estimates - seasonally adjusted
Dataset | Released 8 December 2021
Seasonally adjusted quarterly estimates of life satisfaction, feeling that the things done in life are worthwhile, happiness and anxiety in the UK.

Quarterly personal well-being estimates - non-seasonally adjusted
Dataset | Released 8 December 2021
Non-seasonally adjusted quarterly estimates of life satisfaction, feeling that the things done in life are worthwhile, happiness and anxiety in the UK.

Quality information for quarterly personal well-being estimates
Dataset | Released 8 December 2021
Confidence intervals and sample sizes for quarterly statistics of life satisfaction, feeling that the things done in life are worthwhile, happiness and anxiety in the UK.

4 . Glossary

Personal well-being

Our personal well-being measures ask people to evaluate, on a scale of 0 to 10, how satisfied they are with their life overall, whether they feel they have meaning and purpose in their life, and about their emotions (happiness and anxiety) during a particular period.

Thresholds

Thresholds are used to present the distribution of the data. For the life satisfaction, feeling that things done in life are worthwhile and happiness questions, ratings are grouped in the following way:

- 0 to 4 (low)

- 5 to 6 (medium)

- 7 to 8 (high)

- 9 to 10 (very high)

For the anxiety question, ratings are grouped differently to reflect the fact that higher anxiety is associated with lower personal well-being. The ratings for anxiety are grouped as follows:

- 0 to 1 (very low)

- 2 to 3 (low)

- 4 to 5 (medium)

- 6 to 10 (high)

Coronavirus pandemic timeline

A summary of the context with respect to the coronavirus (COVID-19) pandemic is provided for the period covered by Quarter 4 (Oct to Dec) 2020, Quarter 1 (Jan to Mar) 2021 and Quarter 2 (Apr to June) 2021

Key events during the COVID-19 pandemic – Quarter 4 2020

- Introduction of local restriction tier systems - England: 14 October; Scotland: 2 November.

- National lockdowns - England: 5 November to 2 December; Northern Ireland: 16 October to 11 December; a third lockdown began on 26 December; Wales: 23 October to 9 November.

- Tier 4: "Stay at Home" alert level – introduced in London and South East on 21 December after new coronavirus variant identified in South-East England; Wales: 19 December.

- Reversals of plans to relax restrictions over the Christmas period – 24 November: UK-wide measures for up to three households to meet between 23 to 27 December announced; 19 December: rules tightened to single households and support bubbles.

- Vaccinations - appointments available for those aged 80 years or over, those who are carers and care home residents: 8 December.

Key events during the COVID-19 pandemic – Quarter 1 2021

- National lockdowns – England: 6 January to 29 March (stay-at-home restrictions end); Scotland: lockdown begins 5 January; Wales: stay-at-home restrictions end on 13 March; Northern Ireland: lockdown continues.

- Vaccinations – appointments available in all four nations for frontline health and social care workers, clinically extremely vulnerable and 70 to 79 years age group (January); clinically vulnerable 65 years and over and clinically vulnerable (February); 50 years and over (March).

- Roadmap to stepwise end of lockdowns in all four nations is announced in February and March.

- Mandatory hotel quarantines for those travelling into the UK from "red list" countries introduced from 15 February.

Key events during the COVID-19 pandemic – Quarter 2 2021

- Stay-at-home restrictions end in Scotland (2 April) and Northern Ireland (16 April).

- Relaxation of lockdown restrictions:
    - April to May: non-essential retail, leisure, hairdressers, public buildings and indoor venues open in all four nations

    - May to June: outdoor gatherings of up to 30 people, indoor gathering of up to six people or two households in England, Scotland and Wales; up to 10,000 spectators at outdoor seated venues allowed in England and Wales.

- Vaccinations – appointments available for all aged 40 years and over (April), all aged 30 years and over (May), all adults over 18 years (May to June).

Sources: Institute for Government, Scottish Parliament Information Centre (SPICe), Senedd Research and Northern Ireland Audit Office.

5 . Measuring the data

These quarterly personal well-being estimates are from the Annual Population Survey (APS), which is a continuous household survey covering the UK with the aim of providing estimates between censuses of important social and labour market variables at a local area level.

The figures in this bulletin have been rounded.

The data in this release comes from the APS, which is a different source to that used for the fortnightly well-being figures given in the Coronavirus and the social impacts on Great Britain bulletin. Data for the fortnightly well-being figures come from the Opinions and Lifestyle Survey (OPN), which allows for much more current results. The APS data use a larger sample size and allow for comparison with the back series of data starting in 2011. The estimates will therefore differ slightly for methodological reasons, but the overall trends are the same.

Information on data collection changes because of the coronavirus (COVID-19) pandemic and their impact on estimating personal well-being has been published. The article also outlines why estimates of personal well-being differ between the OPN and the APS.

Quality

More quality and methodology information on strengths, limitations, appropriate uses, and how the data were created is available in the Personal well-being in the UK QMI. For more information on personal well-being, please see the Personal well-being user guidance and Harmonised principles of personal well-being.

6 . Strengths and limitations

Data quality

We first published quarterly data for the personal well-being figures in November 2019 as Experimental Statistics. The aim is to use the quarterly data to explore short-term changes in personal well-being by looking at fluctuation over the years and comparisons over quarters one year apart.

Seasonal adjustment

The data published for our quarterly personal well-being figures are not seasonally adjusted to aid discussion between UK level and non-seasonally adjusted age-splits. Seasonally adjusted estimates at the UK level are available. Seasonal adjustments aid interpretation by removing recurring fluctuations caused, for example, by holidays or other seasonal patterns.

The regARIMA model used to correct the series before applying moving average filters to the seasonal adjustment was reviewed at the end of 2020. There was a slight change to the model, which will be updated in the Personal well-being quarterly estimates technical report.

From reviewing the model, two series within the happiness sub-group were identified as having an Easter effect. The effect was negative for the mean and positive for the "low" happiness threshold series. The implication is that happiness seems to decrease in the period immediately before Easter. More information on this modelling can be found in the Seasonal adjustment methodological note.

Annual Population Survey data reweighting

There has been some data collection changes to the method used for the Annual Population Survey (APS) in response to the coronavirus (COVID-19) pandemic. As a result, the data for this period (October 2020 to April 2021) have a new weighting based on housing tenure. Further information is found in the article Data collection changes because of the coronavirus (COVID-19) pandemic and their impact on estimating personal well-being.

Statistical significance

Please note that:

1. any changes mentioned in this publication are "statistically significant"

2. comparisons have been based on unrounded data

3. the statistical significance of differences noted within the release are determined based on non-overlapping confidence intervals in the unadjusted data

7 . Related links

Personal well-being in the UK: April 2020 to March 2021
Bulletin | Released on 15 October 2021
Estimates of life satisfaction, feeling that the things done in life are worthwhile, happiness and anxiety at the UK, country, regional, county and local authority level.

Personal and economic well-being in Great Britain: May 2021
Bulletin | Released on 25 May 2021
Estimates from multiple sources for personal and economic well-being to understand the economic impact of the coronavirus (COVID-19) pandemic on households in Great Britain from March 2020 to April 2021.

Data collection changes due to the pandemic and their impact on estimating personal well-being
Methodology Technical report | Released on 4 February 2021
During the coronavirus (COVID-19) pandemic, the Office for National Statistics has published estimates of personal well-being using both the Annual Population Survey and the weekly module of the Opinions and Lifestyle Survey. This methodology article considers the impact that the pandemic has had on data collection, how this has influenced estimates of personal well-being and the comparability of these estimates.

Mapping loneliness during the coronavirus pandemic
Article| Released on 7 April 2021
Areas with a higher concentration of younger people and areas with higher rates of unemployment tended to have higher rates of loneliness during the study period.

Statistical bulletin

Social capital in the UK: April 2020 to March 2021

How the UK fared in the four domains of social capital - personal relationships, social network support, civic engagement, and trust and cooperative norms - during April 2020 to March 2021. Sub-population breakdowns by sex, age, ethnicity, disability status, religious status, National Statistics Socio-economic Classification (NS-SEC), urban and rural area, and ITL1 regions are included for the first time in the accompanying data tables.

Contact:
Ida Sadlowska and Eleanor Rees
qualityoflife@ons.gov.uk
+44 1633 455455

Release date:
24 May 2022

Next release:
To be announced

Table of contents

1 . Main points

- Overall, in the UK in 2020 to 2021, the majority of the reviewed social capital indicators remained at their pre-April 2020 levels; however, people's experiences varied depending on their characteristics.

- Females, older people and those in rural areas tend to be more involved in local social and support networks than males, younger people and those in urban areas.

- Females reported having stronger social connections and support links with their local communities than males; 73.6% of females, compared with 65.5% of males, felt that they would receive support from their local community if they needed help during the coronavirus (COVID-19) pandemic (Great Britain, May to August 2020).

- Social network support tends to increase with age; 65.8% of people aged 65 to 74 years checked on their neighbours who might need help compared with 41.3% of those aged 16 to 24 years (Great Britain, May to July 2020).

- Rural areas appear to have stronger community relations than urban areas, although some improvements in social capital in urban communities were observed; the percentage of people who believe that others in general can be trusted increased by 3.9 percentage points in urban areas between 2019 to 2020 and 2020 to 2021 in England.

- Following a period of narrowing, the gender gap in feeling safe when walking alone at night in one's local area increased again to levels seen from 2015 to 2016 through to 2018 to 2019; 69.5% of females reported feeling safe compared with 89.5% of males (England and Wales, 2020 to 2021).

2 . National level social capital over-time

Social capital is a term used to describe the extent and nature of our connections with others and the collective attitudes and behaviours between people that support a well-functioning, close-knit society. This bulletin focuses on social capital across the UK countries, in the context of the first year of the coronavirus (COVID-19) pandemic (April 2020 to March 2021).

Estimates in this bulletin come from several data sources with different geographical coverage and data collection periods. The relevant geographies and time periods are referenced throughout the bulletin. Historical comparisons are provided when available. Differences are assessed using non-overlapping 95% confidence intervals, and only statistically significant differences are reported on. Caution should be exercised when making comparisons between indicators and over time. For more information, see the Measuring the data section.

While most of the social capital indicators did not change significantly in 2020 to 2021 compared with their previous reporting period, in England the percentage of people phoning, or audio or video calling, and the percentage exchanging texts or instant messages with their family and friends at least once a week increased (by 4.1 percentage points and by 2.4 percentage points, respectively). A larger proportion of people also felt that, in general, people can be trusted (2.7 percentage points increase). In contrast, the percentage of people meeting in person with family members or friends at least once a week fell by 7.2 percentage points. The percentage of those engaging in formal volunteering in the last 12 months and those who donated to charity in the last 4 weeks also decreased by 7.3 percentage points and 11.5 percentage points, respectively. Additional research has, however, found an increase in the percentage of people engaging in informal volunteering at least once in the previous 4 weeks.

The observed areas of improvement and deterioration in social capital indicators largely reflect the changes in social interactions related to periods of mandated COVID-19 restrictions.

For the UK, the data collected in March 2021 also show a long-term decrease since 2014 to 2015 in the percentages of people agreeing that others in their neighbourhood can be trusted (a fall of 8.0 percentage points) and that people in their local area are willing to help their neighbours (a fall of 7.2 percentage points). However, as these comparisons are with 2014 to 2015, the changes cannot be solely associated with the most recent years.

Figure 1: While four social capital indicators improved and six deteriorated, the majority of measures remained stable in 2020 to 2021

Assessment of over-time changes in social capital indicators on the national level

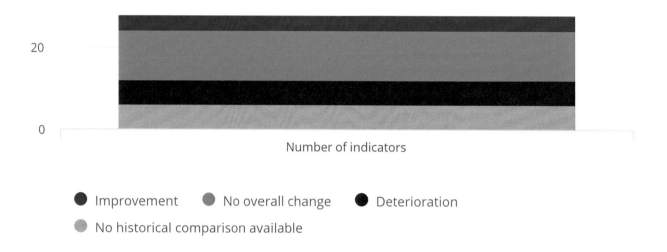

Figure 1: While four social capital indicators improved and six deteriorated, the majority of measures remained stable in 2020 to 2021

Assessment of over-time changes in social capital indicators on the national level

Number of indicators out of the 28 indicators analysed in this release.

Number of indicators

● Improvement   ● No overall change   ● Deterioration

● No historical comparison available

Source: Understanding Society: COVID-19 Study (UK), Understanding Society: The UK Household Longitudinal Study Main Survey (UK), the Opinions and Lifestyle Survey (Great Britain), the Community Life Survey (England), the Telephone-operated Crime Survey for England and Wales and the Crime Survey for England and Wales.

Notes:

1. Over-time comparisons are made to different time periods, depending on the data source and indicator. Latest available pre-April 2020 data were used for each measure.

3 . Social capital by sex

In March 2021 in the UK, comparable percentages of females and males believed that others in their neighbourhood can be trusted (62.1% and 62.0%, respectively) and that people in their local area are willing to help their neighbours (68.2% and 66.6%, respectively). However, females were more likely to be involved in social and support-based interactions in their local areas in the first year of the coronavirus (COVID-19) pandemic.

In Great Britain, between May and August 2020, more females than males declared that they checked on neighbours who might need help at least once in the past seven days (60.8% and 49.7%, respectively). Females were also more likely to feel that they would receive support from their local community if they needed help during the COVID-19 pandemic (73.6% compared with 65.5% of males) (see Figure 2).

Figure 2: Females were more likely than males to check on their neighbours and to believe that they would receive support from their local community in Great Britain in 2020

Percentage of people who checked on neighbours who might need help at least once in the past seven days, by sex, Great Britain, May to July 2020

Percentage of people who believe that other local community members would support them if they needed help during the coronavirus outbreak, by sex, Great Britain, May to August 2020

● Male   ● Female

Percentage of people who checked on neighbours who might need help at least once in the past 7 days

| 40 | 45 | 50 | 55 | 60 | 65 | 70 | 75 | 80 % |

Percentage of people who believe that other local community members would support them if they needed help during the Coronavirus outbreak.

| 40 | 45 | 50 | 55 | 60 | 65 | 70 | 75 | 80 % |

Source: Opinions and Lifestyle Survey - Office for National Statistics

Notes:

1. The estimates are informed by data pooled over two time periods, May to July 2020 (Waves 6 to 19 of the Opinions and Lifestyle Survey) and May to August 2020 (Waves 6 to 21 of the Opinions and Lifestyle Survey), to include the maximum number of survey waves when each question was asked.

2. Question wording for the "Percentage of people who believe that other local community members would support them if they needed help during the coronavirus outbreak" changed slightly for the last two weeks of data collection (Opinions and Lifestyle Survey, Waves 20 and 21) from "If I need help, other local community members would support me during the Coronavirus (COVID-19) outbreak" to "I felt, other local community members would support me during the coronavirus (COVID-19) outbreak".

In March 2021, 29.6% of females in the UK were providing practical help (for example, with shopping, cooking, cleaning, childcare and personal needs) to family, friends or neighbours who were not living in the same household, compared with 22.5% of males (a 7.2 percentage points difference). There was no difference between the percentage of females and males providing financial help to family, friends or neighbours outside their household.

Between 2019 to 2020 and 2020 to 2021, there was a 3.6 percentage points increase in the percentage of females who borrow things and exchange favours with their neighbours in England, from 34.9% to 38.5%. In the same period, the percentage of females who believed that in general most people can be trusted increased in England, from 60.6% to 64.4%, while there was no change for men. More females than males also reported feeling that they belong to their neighbourhood (66.3% and 63.1%, respectively) in 2020 to 2021.

Despite females' improving neighbourhood connections, the Telephone-operated Crime Survey for England and Wales (TCSEW) estimated that the percentage of females declaring that they felt safe walking alone in their local area after dark levelled at 69.5% in 2020 to 2021. In contrast, the percentage of males who felt safe increased by 2.7 percentage points, from 86.8% to 89.5%. This led to widening of the gender gap in feelings of safety between 2019 to 2020 and 2020 to 2021 (please note the change in survey methodology in 2020 to 2021, which might have affected the estimates). This widening follows a period of narrowing observed in the estimates from the Crime Survey for England and Wales (CSEW) between 2015 to 2016 and 2019 to 2020, when the percentage of females feeling safe increased while the percentage of males feeling safe remained stable (see Figure 3). More recent analysis of perceptions of personal safety and experiences of harassment in Great Britain is also available on the ONS website, with data for February to March 2022 available from 25 May 2022.

Figure 3: The gap between the percentage of females and males reporting feeling safe walking alone in their local area after dark increased in England and Wales between 2019 to 2020 and 2020 to 2021

Percentage of females and males who felt "very" or "fairly" safe walking alone in their local area after dark, England and Wales, between 2015 to 2016 and 2020 to 2021

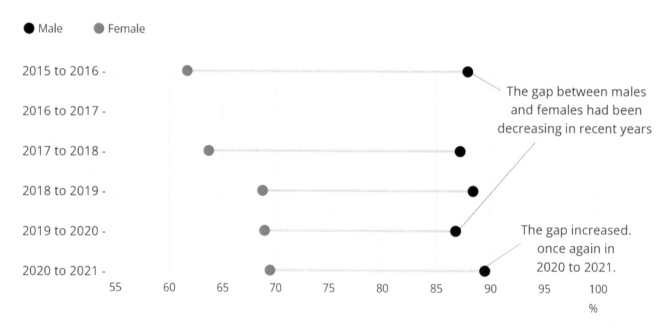

Source: Telephone-operated Crime Survey for England and Wales - Office for National Statistics and Crime Survey for England and Wales - Office for National Statistics

Notes:

1. The methodology of data collection changed in 2020 to 2021, compared with the previous years. The 2020 to 2021 data were collected between May 2020 and March 2021 using the Telephone-operated Crime Survey for England and Wales (TCSEW). The data for earlier time periods were collected in face-to-face interviews as part of the Crime Survey for England and Wales (CSEW).

2. ONS guidance explains comparability between the TCSEW and the face-to-face CSEW.

3. The TCSEW estimates for 2020 to 2021 will differ from those previously published for this period because only data collected in Wave 1 interviews were presented for comparability purposes.

4. The CSEW estimates for 2019 to 2020 will not match those previously published as those aged 16 to 17 years have been removed for comparability.

5. There may be some overlap of interviews between the 2019 to 2020 data and the 2020 to 2021 data.

4 . Social capital by age

During 2020 to 2021 in England, all age groups reported a decrease in frequency of in-person meetings with family and friends, in line with restrictions related to the coronavirus (COVID-19) pandemic at the time. The decrease was most substantial for those aged 16 to 24 years (9.4 percentage points), those aged 65 to 74 years (9.8 percentage points) and those aged 75 years and over (8.9 percentage points), when compared with 2019 to 2020 (see Figure 4).

Figure 4: People in all age groups reported meeting up in person with family and friends less in England in 2020 to 2021 compared with 2019 to 2020

Percentage of people who meet up in person with family members or friends at least once a week, by age, England, 2019 to 2020 and 2020 to 2021

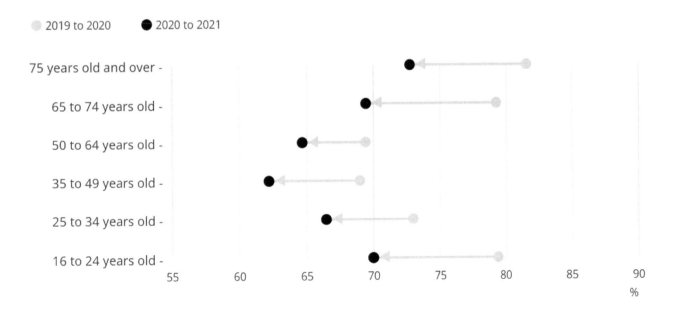

Source: Community Life Survey - Department for Digital, Culture, Media and Sport

Those aged 16 to 24 years were the only age group for which a substantial increase (11.2 percentage points) was observed in the percentage of people involved in civic activism (contacting local officials, attending a rally or signing a petition) in England in 2020 to 2021. This may be a temporary increase caused by high-profile societal events, such as racial injustice protests and climate change protests, Brexit, and cases of violence against women and girls, but it could also be an early sign of a more general change in young people's involvement in civic matters.

In terms of involvement in support relations, in March 2021 in the United Kingdom, 36.5% of those aged 50 to 64 years reported giving practical help (for example, with shopping, cooking, cleaning, childcare and personal needs) to family, friends or neighbours who did not live with them (see Figure 5). Those in age groups above 50 years old were also more likely than those aged under 50 years to give financial assistance to their family, friends or neighbours. These findings give an insight into a unique "burden of care" that these groups might have experienced during the COVID-19 pandemic. Among those receiving support, those aged 65 to 74 years and 75 years and over were less likely to receive financial support (2.0% and 2.3%, respectively), but they were more likely to receive practical support (18.8% and 30.5%, respectively) than the younger age groups.

Figure 5: Those aged 50 to 64 years were most likely to provide practical support to others in the UK in March 2021

Percentage of people who in the last four weeks provided practical help to family, friends or neighbours who do not live with them, by age, UK, March 2021

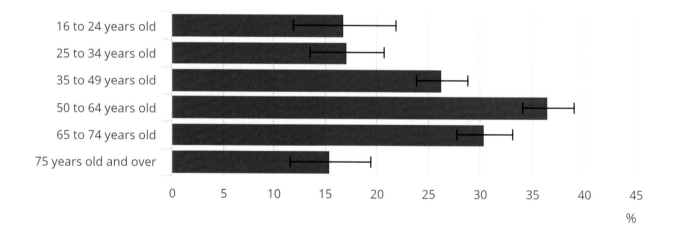

Figure 5: Those aged 50 to 64 years were most likely to provide practical support to others in the UK in March 2021

Percentage of people who in the last four weeks provided practical help to family, friends or neighbours who do not live with them, by age, UK, March 2021

Source: Understanding Society: COVID-19 Study Wave 8

The older age groups also reported feeling more connected to neighbourhood support networks than those in the younger age groups. In Great Britain in May to August 2020, 65.8% of people aged 65 to 74 years were checking on their neighbours who might need help, compared with 41.3% of those aged 16 to 24 years. Similarly, 84.7% of those aged 75 and over believed that they would be supported by other local community members during the COVID-19 pandemic, compared with 58.1% of those aged 25 to 34 years (see Figure 6). This age-based pattern may help contextualise findings from other Office for National Statistics (ONS) research, which showed that younger people were more likely to have had their well-being affected by the coronavirus than the elderly.

Figure 6: Rates of involvement in neighbourhood and local community support networks (relying on neighbours for support and checking on neighbours) were greater among the older age groups in Great Britain in 2020

Percentage of people who checked on neighbours who might need help at least once in the past seven days, by age, Great Britain, May to July 2020

Percentage of people who believe that other local community members would support them if they needed help during the coronavirus outbreak, by age, Great Britain, May to August 2020

Percentage of people who checked on neighbours who might need help at least once in the past 7 days

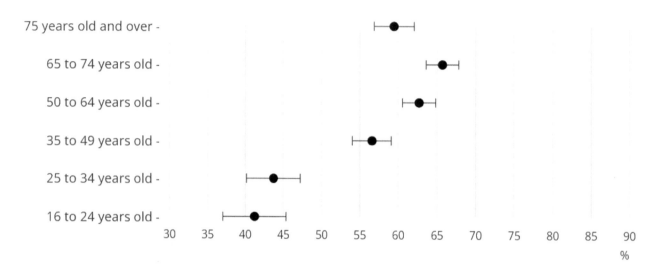

Percentage of people who believe that other local community members would support them if they needed help during the Coronavirus outbreak

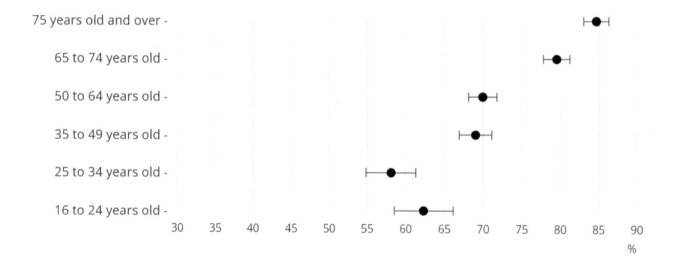

Source: Opinions and Lifestyle Survey - Office for National Statistics

Notes:

1. The estimates are informed by data pooled over two time periods, May to July 2020 (Waves 6 to 19 of the Opinions and Lifestyle Survey) and May to August 2020 (Waves 6 to 21 of the Opinions and Lifestyle Survey), to include the maximum number of survey waves when each question was asked.

2. Question wording for the "Percentage of people who believe that other local community members would support them if they needed help during the coronavirus outbreak" changed slightly for the last two weeks of data collection (Opinions and Lifestyle Survey, Waves 20 and 21) from "If I need help, other local community members would support me during the coronavirus (COVID-19) outbreak" to "I felt, other local community members would support me during the coronavirus (COVID-19) outbreak".

5 . Social capital by urban and rural area

In England in 2020 to 2021, larger percentages of people in rural areas reported talking regularly with their neighbours (81.8% compared with 72.4% of the urban population) and borrowing things or exchanging favours (44.1% compared with 35.6% of the urban population). These area-based differences were observed both in 2019 to 2020 and 2020 to 2021, with no over-time changes for either of the areas.

In addition, between May and July 2020 in Great Britain, 63.8% of people in rural areas were checking on their neighbours who might need help, compared with 53.2% of those in urban areas. More people in rural areas, than in urban areas, also felt that they could rely on their local community for support (79.3% and 67.4%, respectively).

In March 2021 in the UK, 75.4% of people in rural areas agreed that people in their area are willing to help their neighbours (compared with 65.0% of those in urban areas).

While people in rural areas appear to have stronger social network support than those in urban areas, our data show over-time improvements in the urban-rural gap in levels of trust and cooperative norms (see Figure 7). In England in 2020 to 2021, the gap in the sense of belonging to one's neighbourhood narrowed down from 11.1 percentage points (in 2019 to 2020) to 8.3 percentage points between those in rural and urban areas. At the same time, the gap in generalised trust levels decreased from 15.6 percentage points to 9.1 percentage points because of an increase in the percentage of urban people who think that people in general can be trusted. Finally, while the neighbourhood trust levels (percentage of people agreeing that most people in their neighbourhood can be trusted) fell sharply in both rural and urban areas between 2014 to 2015 and March 2021, they declined more in the rural communities. As a result, the urban-rural gap in neighbourhood trust also narrowed from 14.2 percentage points to 10.9 percentage points.

Figure 7: Gaps in sense of neighbourhood belonging, generalised trust levels and neighbourhood trust levels between urban and rural areas narrowed in 2020 to 2021

Percentage of people who feel strongly that they belong to their neighbourhood, by area type, England, 2020 to 2021

Percentage of people who think that people in general can be trusted, by area type, England, 2020 to 2021

Percentage of people who would say that most people in their neighbourhood can be trusted, by area type, UK, March 2021

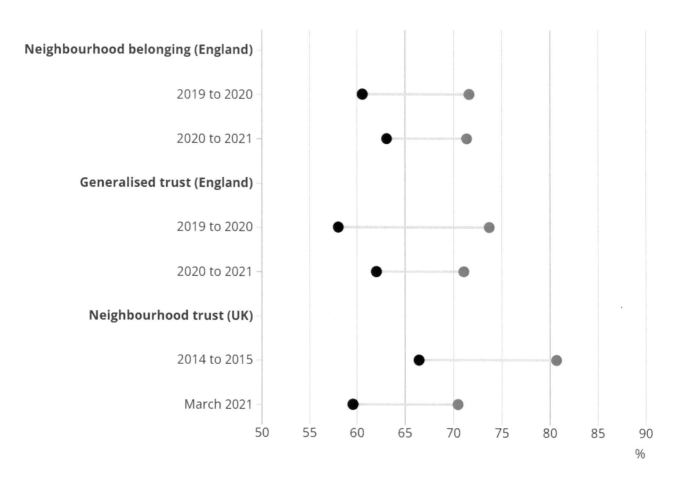

Source: Community Life Survey - Department for Digital, Culture, Media & Sport, Understanding Society: COVID-19 Study and Understanding Society: The UK Longitudinal Household Study Main Survey

Notes:

1. The estimates presented on the chart come from data sources with differing coverage of time periods and geographies so should not be directly compared.

2. For neighbourhood trust, the comparisons are with 2014 to 2015, and therefore the changes cannot be solely associated with the most recent years.

In urban areas, there was also a 2.8 percentage points increase (from 85.2% to 88.0%) in the percentage of males reporting feeling safe walking alone after dark in their local area in England and Wales between 2019 to 2020 and 2020 to 2021 (please note the change in survey methodology between 2019 to 2020 and 2020 to 2021, which might have affected the estimates). No change was seen in urban females' feelings of safety. In 2020 to 2021, females in urban areas continued to feel safe at a below average rate of 66.6% (compared with 69.5% of all females and 81.4% of females in rural areas) (see Figure 8). The gender gap in feelings of safety increased in both urban and rural areas since 2019 to 2020 and remained bigger in urban areas (21.5 percentage points) than in rural areas (14.6 percentage points) in 2020 to 2021.

Figure 8: Females in urban areas reported the lowest rates of feeling safe walking alone in their local area after dark (for estimates by sex and area type) in England and Wales in 2020 to 2021.

Percentages of females and males who felt "very" or "fairly" safe walking alone in their local area after dark, England and Wales, May 2020 to March 2021

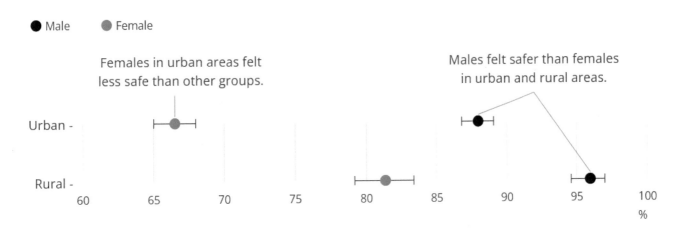

Source: Telephone-operated Crime Survey for England and Wales - Office for National Statistics

Notes:

1. The methodology of data collection for the Crime Survey for England and Wales changed in 2020 to 2021, compared with the previous years, from face-to-face interviews to telephone interviews.

2. The Telephone-operated Crime Survey for England and Wales estimates for 2020 to 2021 will differ from those previously published for this period because only data collected in Wave 1 interviews were presented for comparability

6 . Social capital in the UK data

Social capital headline indicators
Dataset | Released 24 May 2022
Current headline indicators of social capital in the UK. This dataset includes data collected between April 2020 and March 2021 for each indicator with a comparison with latest pre-April 2020 data where available. Sub-population breakdowns by sex, age, ethnicity, disability status, religious status, National Statistics Socio-economic Classification (NS-SEC), urban and rural area, and ITL1 regions are included where available.

7 . Glossary

Social capital

Social capital is a term used to describe the extent and nature of our connections with others and the collective attitudes and behaviours between people that support a well-functioning, close-knit society.

Personal relationships

This aspect of social capital refers to the structure and nature of people's personal relationships and is concerned with who people know and what they do to establish and maintain their personal relationships.

Social network support

This aspect of social capital refers to the level of resources or support that a person can draw from their personal relationships, but also includes what people do for other individuals on a personal basis.

Civic engagement

This aspect of social capital refers to the actions and behaviours that can be seen as contributing positively to the collective life of a community or society. It includes activities such as volunteering, political participation and other forms of community actions.

Trust and cooperative norms

This aspect of social capital refers to the trust and cooperative norms or shared values that are beneficial for the society as a whole and which shape the way people behave towards each other and as members of society.

8 . Measuring the data

Social capital indicators

This release focuses on measuring social capital in the UK between April 2020 and March 2021. The selection of analysed indicators is based on the framework of 25 headline measures of social capital proposed by the Office for National Statistics (ONS) in 2015, and reported on in 2017 and 2020. However, to ensure data availability for 2020 to 2021, we could not use all original indicators and data sources. Given this release's focus on the coronavirus (COVID-19) pandemic, we have also included some new indicators.

This release's commentary focuses on a selection of indicators and demographic and geographic sub-groups. The full set of social capital estimates and breakdowns, and the full list of indicator changes are available in the accompanying data tables.

Data coverage

The data in this release come from several data sources and have been collected at various times between April 2020 and March 2021. As a result, the estimates are relevant for different countries of the UK and different time periods during 2020 to 2021 (see Data sources in Measuring the data section). Historical comparisons with the latest pre-April 2020 data are provided where available, but their timeliness also varies. In addition, for some of the data sources (for example, the Crime Survey for England and Wales), the mode of data collection changed in 2020 to 2021, compared with pre-April 2020. Therefore, caution should be exercised when making comparisons over-time and between indicators.

All analysed data were known to be current as of 4 January 2022.

Data sources

The following surveys informed this release:

- Understanding Society: COVID-19 Study, March 2021 (Wave 8), UK.

- Understanding Society: UK Household Longitudinal Study Main Survey, the 2014 to 2015 (Wave 6, UK) and 2018 to 2019 (Wave 10, UK) for historical comparison data

- the Opinions and Lifestyle Survey (OPN) May to July 2020 (Waves 6 to 19, Great Britain) for the "Checking on neighbours" indicator

- the Opinions and Lifestyle Survey (OPN) May to August 2020 (Waves 6 to 21, Great Britain) for the "Community support" indicator

- the Community Life Survey (CLS), April 2020 to March 2021 (England)

- the Community Life Survey (CLS), April 2019 to March 2020 (England) for historical comparison data

- the Telephone-operated Crime Survey for England and Wales (TCSEW), May 2020 to March 2021 (England and Wales)

- the Crime Survey for England and Wales (CSEW), April 2019 to March 2020 (England and Wales) for historical comparison data

Please note that for the Crime Survey for England and Wales, the survey methodology changed in 2020 to 2021 from face-to-face interviews to telephone-based interviews. Further information on comparability between the Telephone-operated Crime Survey for England and Wales and the Crime Survey for England and Wales can be found on the ONS website.

No historical comparisons are available for the Opinions and Lifestyle Survey.

Analysis and methodology

The social capital estimates are based on cross-sectional survey data. This means that survey data were collected for a sample of the population of interest at a point in time, and then weighted to adjust the estimates for representativeness of the population. Therefore, the estimates are subject to uncertainty, which is expressed using 95% confidence intervals. The ONS guidance on uncertainty contains more information on how we measure and communicate uncertainty for survey data.

In this release, over-time changes and differences between sub-populations are only commented on if they are statistically significant using non-overlapping 95% confidence intervals. This is a conservative method of assessing change, so it is possible that significant differences that have not been identified using this method exist in the data.

All analysis has been done on unrounded figures. Some figures may not sum because of rounding.

Social capital in the devolved administrations

Several indicators presented in this release are not currently measured at the UK level. For the indicators where the UK-wide data are not available, alternative data sources may exist for the devolved nations, but differences in methodology may affect comparability of the data.

For more information about social capital data collected by the devolved administrations, see the Related links section.

Improving measures of social capital

In July 2021, the ONS published the Social capital harmonised standard, which sets out how to collect and report social capital indicators to improve comparability across different data sources. The standard provides a set of six social capital questions, which were determined to best capture the underlying concepts of the ONS social capital framework.

9 . Strengths and limitations

The main limitation of the presented social capital data is their coverage of geographies and time periods. We prioritised data sources that collected data between April 2020 and March 2021. Therefore, estimates are not always relevant for all of the UK, some indicators are only representative for a specific period between April 2020 and March 2021, and historical comparisons are not available for several indicators.

The main strength of this release is the sub-population breakdowns by demographic characteristics and geographies, which have been included for the first time. These additional breakdowns uncovered demographic patterns in the levels of social capital in the UK, resulting in more comprehensive and detailed insights. Still, certain suspected over-time changes and cross-group differences could not be established as the estimates for smaller sub-groups have higher levels of uncertainty because of the limited sample sizes.

10 . Related links

Social capital harmonised standard
Standard | Released 13 July 2021
The social capital harmonised standard sets out how to collect and report social capital statistics to ensure comparability across different data sources. The standard outlines a set of six essential social capital questions with appropriate answer options. The questions were developed through principal component analysis and discussions with an expert topic group, and they were determined to best capture the underlying concepts of the Office for National Statistics' social capital framework. They were cognitively tested in February 2021 and are recommended to users aiming to measure social capital in surveys.

Measuring Social Capital
Article | Released 18 July 2014
The original list of headline measures proposed by the Office for National Statistics (ONS) using a framework that covers the four core domains of social capital: personal relationships, social network support, civic engagement, and trust and cooperative norms. Defines social capital and highlights some examples of the importance of measuring it.

Four interpretations of social capital: an agenda for measurement
Working paper | Released 10 December 2013
An Organisation for Economic Co-operation and Development (OECD) paper that clarifies the range of different elements that are encompassed by the term "social capital", discusses the measurement issues, and makes recommendations for future research and the establishment of comparative social capital measures.

Crime in England and Wales: Annual supplementary tables
Dataset | Released 17 July 2020
Data tables providing (in Table S37) the long-term data on females' and males' feelings of safety when walking alone in their local area after dark from January to December 1994 until April 2019 to March 2020.

Northern Ireland - CHS Social Capital
Dataset | Released 15 March 2017
The Northern Ireland Statistics and Research Agency's (NISRA's) latest social capital data from the Continuous Household Survey (CHS). The survey asks questions on a variety of topics, such as internet access, the environment, tourism, libraries, health, sport and education. Northern Ireland also publishes estimates for some of the measures of social capital, including measures of loneliness and volunteering in annual reports by The Executive Office and The Department for Communities.

Scotland - National Indicator Performance
Web page | Live page
An overview from the Scottish Government of how Scotland is performing against 81 National Indicators, which include a Social Capital Index. The index monitors aggregate changes in levels of social capital in Scotland since 2013 through the four domains of social networks, community cohesion, community empowerment and social participation.

Wales - Wellbeing of Wales: national indicators
Web page | Released 15 December 2021
An overview from the Welsh Government of performance against Welsh national wellbeing indicators and national wellbeing goals. Indicators include social capital measures such as rates of loneliness, volunteering and feeling able to influence decisions affecting the local area. Wales also collects and publishes some social capital data in reports from the National Survey for Wales

Quality of life in the UK: August 2022

An overview of UK's progress across ten domains of national well-being – personal well-being, relationships, health, what we do, where we live, personal finance, economy, education and skills, governance, and environment. This bulletin provides the first update to the Measures of National Well-being dashboard since 2019.

Contact:

Ida Sadlowska and Eleanor Rees

Release date:

12 August 2022

Next release:

To be announced

Table of contents

1. Main points

- Levels of personal well-being deteriorated during the coronavirus (COVID-19) pandemic, and in January to March 2022 continued to remain below their pre-coronavirus (October to December 2019) levels.

- In June to July 2022, people in Great Britain reported high levels of social capital; 86.8% of adults agreed that they can rely on people in their life if they have a serious problem, while 66.1% declared that in general they trust most people.

- Sports participation rates changed in May 2020 to May 2021, compared with earlier time-periods; 60.9% of adults in England reported participating in moderate intensity sport or physical activity for at least 150 minutes a week, a decline since May 2019 to May 2020 (62.8%).

- At the end of 2021, after almost two years of the coronavirus pandemic and the associated increases in public spending, the UK's public sector net debt reached 97.3% of Gross Domestic Product, the highest value since the early 1960's.

- Greenhouse gas emissions continued to decrease in the UK in 2020, with an estimated 405.5 MtCO2e emitted (compared with 447.9 MtCO2e in 2019); this decrease was related to the reduction in production and transport during coronavirus and was not sustained in 2021 (provisional 2021 estimate: 424.5 MtCO2e).

- This bulletin is accompanied by the Measures of National Well-being Dashboard: Quality of Life in the UK (https://www.ons.gov.uk/peoplepopulationandcommunity/wellbeing/articles/measureso fnationalwellbeingdashboardqualityoflifeintheuk/2022-08-12).

 Estimates are from different data sources and therefore are representative for different geographies and time periods. Therefore, caution is advised when making comparisons between indicators and over time. The impact of the coronavirus pandemic on data collection and people's opinions should also be considered. For more detail on

data sources, see <u>Section 15: Measuring the data</u>

<u>(https://www.ons.gov.uk/peoplepopulationandcommunity/wellbeing/bulletins/quali</u>

<u>tyoflifeintheuk/august2022#measuring-the-data</u>)**.**

2. Personal well-being

Personal (subjective) well-being of individuals is central to understanding national well-being (see Section 14: Glossary (https://www.ons.gov.uk/peoplepopulationandcommunity/wellbeing/bulletins/qualityoflifein theuk/august2022#glossary)).

> **⚠ Personal well-being data presented for the periods Quarter 1 (Jan to Mar) 2020 to Quarter 2 (Apr to June) 2021, sourced from the Annual Population Survey datasets year ending March 2020 to year ending June 2021, are affected by an error in the calculation of population weights. This affects the age breakdown of the population in Wales to a small extent. Breakdowns for the UK as a whole would be largely unaffected. We aim to explore the extent of this error on personal well-being estimates and revise them as necessary in September 2022.**

In January to March 2022, 25.5% of adults aged 16 years and over in the UK reported a very high level of overall life satisfaction, while 32.2% reported a very high level of feeling that the things they do are worthwhile. For emotions felt the previous day, 30.5% of people rated their happiness as very high and 34.1% reported having felt very low levels of anxiety.

In January to March 2022, the four measures of personal well-being continued to remain below their pre-coronavirus (COVID-19) levels and the levels in January to March 2017, showing long-term deterioration in personal well-being in the UK (Figure 1).

However, there were short-term improvements since January to March 2021 with people reporting very high life satisfaction (an increase from 21.7% to 25.5%) and very high levels of happiness (an increase from 27.6% to 30.5%). The percentage of people reporting very high feeling that things they do in life are worthwhile and very low levels of anxiety remained stable from the previous year.

Figure 1: In January to March 2022, the four measures of personal well-being continued to remain below their pre-coronavirus levels (October to December 2019)

Percentage of adults giving a very high rating of their life satisfaction, whether they feel the things they do in life are worthwhile and happiness, and a very low rating of anxiety, UK, April 2011 to March 2022

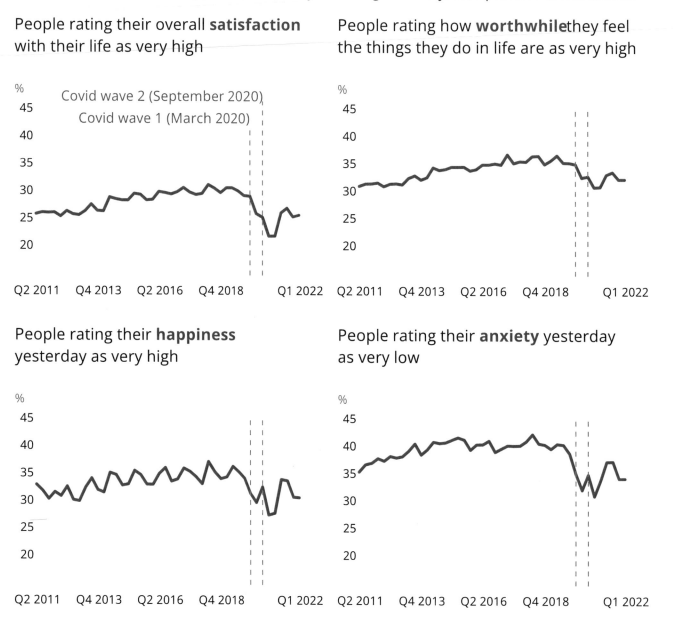

People rating their overall **satisfaction** with their life as very high

People rating how **worthwhile** they feel the things they do in life are as very high

People rating their **happiness** yesterday as very high

People rating their **anxiety** yesterday as very low

Source: Annual Population Survey - Office for National Statistics

Embed code

Notes:

1. Questions: "Overall, how satisfied are you with your life nowadays?", "Overall, to what extent do you feel that the things you do in your life are worthwhile?", "Overall, how happy did you feel yesterday?", and "Overall, how anxious did you feel yesterday?"

2. Questions are answered on a scale of 0 to 10, where 0 is "not at all" and 10 is "completely".

3. Very high estimates of life satisfaction, whether you feel the things you do in life are worthwhile and happiness are defined as answering 9 or 10 out of 10. Very low estimates of anxiety are defined as answering 0 or 1 out of 10.

4. For more information, see Personal well-being user guidance (https://www.ons.gov.uk/peoplepopulationandcommunity/wellbeing/methodologies/personalwellbeingsurveyuserguide).

Download the data

.xlsx (https://www.ons.gov.uk/visualisations/dvc2102/fig1/wrapper/datadownload.xlsx)

A more detailed analysis of the changes in personal well-being levels since the beginning of the coronavirus pandemic can be found in our Personal well-being in the UK, quarterly Statistical bulletin series (https://www.ons.gov.uk/peoplepopulationandcommunity/wellbeing/bulletins/personalwellbeingintheukquarterly/previousReleases).

For fortnightly estimates of personal well-being, see our Public opinions and social trends, Great Britain Statistical bulletin series (https://www.ons.gov.uk/peoplepopulationandcommunity/wellbeing/bulletins/publicopinionsandsocialtrendsgreatbritain/previousReleases).

3. Our relationships

People's relationships have an impact on their well-being outcomes, including quality of life and happiness.

In the UK, 4.3% of adults aged 16 years and over reported they were fairly or extremely unhappy with their relationship in January 2019 to December 2020. This represents a long-term improvement (decline), with the percentage of adults in unhappy relationships almost halving compared with 8.3% in January 2013 to December 2014. Following the peaks in January 2011 to December 2012 and January 2013 to December 2014, the percentage of adults in unhappy relationships has declined and remained stable since January 2015.

The percentage of adults feeling lonely often or always remained stable in recent years. In 2020 to 2021, 6.5% of adults aged 16 years and over in England reported feeling lonely often or always, no short-term change compared with 2019 to 2020 (6.4%). The incremental increase from 5.4% in 2016 to 2017 was not statistically significant (Figure 2).

Figure 2: The percentage of people reporting they were unhappy with their relationships and the percentage of people who felt lonely often or always have been generally stable in recent years

Percentage of people in fairly or extremely unhappy relationships, UK, 2015 to 2016 until 2019 to 2020, and the percentage of people who feel lonely often or always, England, 2016 to 2017 to 2020 to 2021

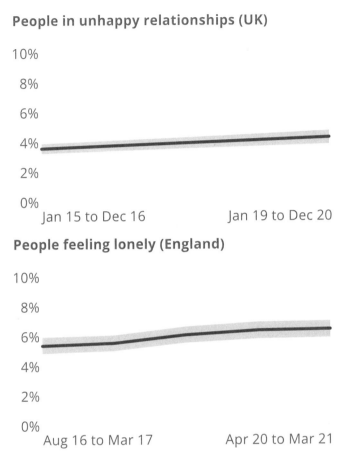

People in unhappy relationships (UK)

People feeling lonely (England)

Source: Understanding Society: The UK Household Longitudinal Study and Community Life Survey - Department for Culture, Media & Sport

Embed code

In terms of relationships with social support networks and communities, people in Great Britain appear to feel well connected. In June to July 2022, 86.8% of adults aged 16 years and over in Great Britain strongly agreed or agreed that they can rely on people in their life if they have a serious problem. In the same period, 66.1% of adults declared that in general they trust most people. These are both metrics of social capital. High levels of social capital support a well-functioning society and can be expected to support national well-being. For more information, see our Social capital in the UK: April 2020 to March 2021 bulletin (https://www.ons.gov.uk/peoplepopulationandcommunity/wellbeing/bulletins/socialcapitalintheuk/latest).

For fortnightly estimates of loneliness for Great Britain, see our Public opinions and social trends, Great Britain Statistical bulletin series (https://www.ons.gov.uk/peoplepopulationandcommunity/wellbeing/bulletins/publicopinionsandsocialtrendsgreatbritain/previousReleases).

4. Health

An individual's physical and mental health is an important component of their overall well-being.

(!) **The latest data available for this domain are representative for 2018, 2019 and 2020. At present, any potential impact of the coronavirus (COVID-19) pandemic on health indicators cannot be evaluated.**

In 2018 to 2020, the average healthy life expectancy at birth was estimated at 63.6 years for females and 62.8 years for males in the UK. Between 2011 and 2020, healthy life expectancy remained relatively stable for both males and females at the UK level, with females having longer healthy life expectancy than males. However, further socio-economic and geographical inequalities in healthy life expectancy exist in the UK (see our Health state life expectancies, UK: 2018 to 2020 bulletin (https://www.ons.gov.uk/peoplepopulationandcommunity/healthandsocialcare/healthandlifeexpectancies/bulletins/healthstatelifeexpectanciesuk/2018to2020)).

While this suggests that on the whole the UK population's lifetime health did not change, other indicators show that people's current health-related well-being varied over time.

In 2019 to 2020, 46.9% of people reported being mostly or completely satisfied with their health. No change has been observed over the short term (47.8% in 2018 to 2019), but the health satisfaction levels deteriorated over the long term (49.6% in 2014 to 2015). Although the health satisfaction levels remained stable between 2017 and 2020, the percentage of people reporting some evidence of depression or anxiety increased (Figure 3).

In 2019 to 2020, 21.8% of people reported some evidence of depression or anxiety, the highest rate since the beginning of data collection in 2009 to 2010. This represents a deterioration (increase) over the short term (19.8% in 2018 to 2019) and the long term (17.4% in 2014 to 2015).

Figure 3: The percentage of people satisfied with their health remained unchanged since 2018, while the percentage of people reporting some evidence of depression or anxiety increased over the same period

Percentage of people who are mostly or completely satisfied with their health, and the percentage of people reporting some evidence of depression or anxiety, UK, 2014 to 2015 until 2019 to 2020

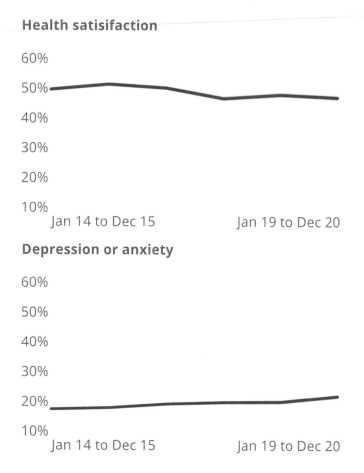

Source: Understanding Society: The UK Household Longitudinal Study.

Embed code

Download the data

.xlsx (https://www.ons.gov.uk/visualisations/dvc2102/fig3wrapper/datadownload.xlsx)

More recent analysis on the prevalence of depressive symptoms among adults in Great Britain during the coronavirus pandemic can be found in our Coronavirus and depression in adults in Great Britain article series (https://www.ons.gov.uk/peoplepopulationandcommunity/wellbeing/articles/coronavirusanddepressioninadultsgreatbritain/previousReleases).

5. What we do

Participation in and satisfaction with work and leisure activities influences people's well-being, lifestyles and relationships.

In March to May 2022, the unemployment rate was estimated at 3.8% in the UK. This represents a short-term improvement (decrease) compared with 4.9% in March to May 2021, and a long-term improvement from 4.4% in March to May 2017. During the coronavirus (COVID-19) pandemic, the unemployment rate rose above 5% between August 2020 and February 2021 but returned to the pre-coronavirus (December 2019 to February 2020) levels by October to December 2021. These fluctuations are coupled with changes in labour market inactivity and vacancy rates, and are explored in our Labour market overview: July 2022 bulletin (https://www.ons.gov.uk/employmentandlabourmarket/peopleinwork/employmentandempl oyeetypes/bulletins/uklabourmarket/previousReleases).

For leisure participation, in May 2020 to May 2021, 60.9% of adults aged 16 years and over in England reported participating in moderate intensity sport or physical activity for an average of at least 150 minutes a week (the NHS recommendation for adults). This represents a short-term decline since 2019 to 2020 (62.8%) and is the lowest rate recorded since 2016 to 2017 (Figure 4). However, this may be explained by data collection coinciding with periods of heightened coronavirus infection rates and restrictions.

Figure 4: In 2020 to 2021, the rate of participation in moderate intensity sport or physical activity in England has been the lowest since 2016 to 2017

Percentage of adults who on average take part in moderate intensity sport or physical activity for at least 150 minutes a week, England, May 2016 to May 2017 to May 2020 to May 2021

Source: Sports England – Active Lives Survey

Notes:

1. Moderate intensity activity is defined as an activity which raises heart rate; most sports and physical activities are included (aside from gardening).

2. Bouts of 10 or more minutes of activity are added up to average weekly activity levels.

3. Moderate intensity activity of 150 minutes a week is the NHS recommended amount for adults.

In October 2021 to March 2022, 86.8% of adults aged 16 years and over in England declared that they engaged with the arts sector in person in the last 12 months. In June to July 2022, 29.2% of adults aged 16 years and over in Great Britain reported that they volunteered (gave unpaid help to clubs, groups, charities or organisations) in the previous 12 months, and 58.9% reported doing so at least once a month.

While people's involvement in work and leisure activities was disrupted by coronavirus, it is worth noting that sustained levels of job and leisure satisfaction were observed pre-coronavirus until 2019 to 2020. In 2019 to 2020, in the UK, 58.4% of adults aged 16 years and over declared being mostly or completely satisfied with their current job, while 45.0% reported being mostly or completely satisfied with the amount of leisure time they have. The percentages of people satisfied with their job and leisure time remained unchanged over the short term, compared with 2018 to 2019. However, job satisfaction has been improving incrementally over the long term since 2013 to 2014. The percentage of people satisfied with their leisure time increased between 2013 to 2014 and 2014 to 2015, but there was no long-term change between 2014 to 2015 (44.7%) and 2019 to 2020 (45.0%).

6. Where we live

Where people live, the quality of their local area and their community, and how they feel about it can have a significant impact on the well-being of individuals.

In the year ending March 2020, the personal crime incidence rate was estimated at 49.8 offences per 1,000 adults in England and Wales. This represents a long-term improvement (decrease) compared with an estimated 65.9 crimes per 1,000 adults in the year ending March 2015, a reduction by more than two-fifths from the year ending March 2011 (Figure 5).

Patterns of crime over the last two years have been affected substantially by the coronavirus (COVID-19) pandemic and government restrictions on social contacts. While periods of national lockdown have seen decreases in the incidence of many types of crime, fraud and computer misuse offences have increased substantially. Estimates from the Telephone Crime Survey for England and Wales for the year ending March 2022 compared with the pre-coronavirus year ending March 2020 showed no statistically significant change in total crime.

Figure 5: Incidence rates of personal crime have been falling in England and Wales between the year ending March 2011 and the year ending March 2020.

Incidence of personal crime, England and Wales, April 2010 to March 2011 until April 2019 to March 2020

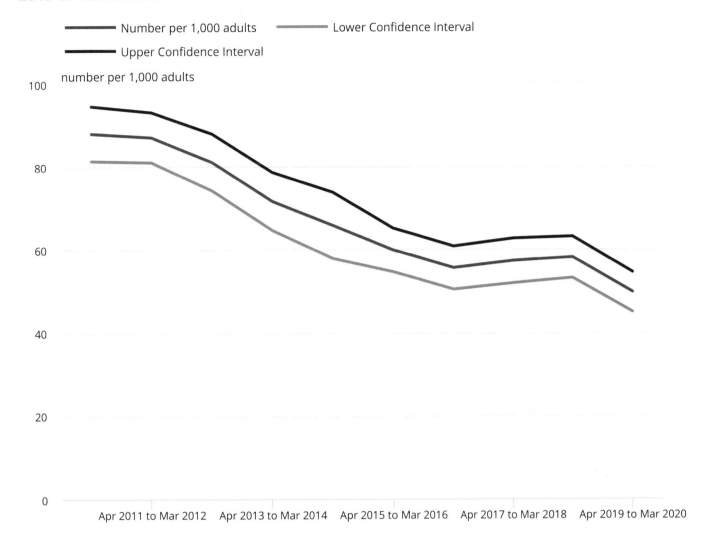

Source: Office for National Statistics – Crime Survey for England and Wales

Notes:

1. Presented estimates are based on data collected from face-to-face interviews using the Crime Survey for England and Wales (CSEW). The methodology of data collection changed during the coronavirus pandemic, and from May 2020 onwards data have been collected using the Telephone-operated Crime Survey for England and Wales (TCSEW). Data on personal crime incidence collected using TCSEW are not directly comparable with those presented in this bulletin and have not been included. The Office for National Statistics' guidance explains comparability between the face-to-face CSEW and the TCSEW

(https://www.ons.gov.uk/peoplepopulationandcommunity/crimeandjustice/methodolog ies/comparabilitybetweenthetelephoneoperatedcrimesurveyforenglandandwalesandth efacetofacecrimesurveyforenglandandwales).

In the year ending March 2022, 67.7% of females and 91.1% of males in England and Wales reported feeling very or fairly safe when walking alone after dark in their local area. This represents no short-term change for either females or males since the year ending March 2021 (69.5% and 89.5%, respectively).

For accessibility of local spaces, 60.9% of people in England reported that they accessed the natural environment in the last 14 days in March 2022. This represents no short-term change when compared with March 2021 (63.2%). Between June 2020 and March 2022, the percentage of people visiting the natural environment remained generally stable. April 2020 (the first month of data collection, and the beginning of the coronavirus pandemic and the first national lockdown) saw the lowest proportion of people (49.0%) reporting accessing the natural environment.

7. Personal finance

How households and individuals are managing financially influences their life satisfaction, happiness and anxiety levels.

⊘ **The estimates in this domain are representative for periods up to March 2021. Therefore, more recent changes to people's financial well-being are not covered in this bulletin.**

In the financial year ending March 2021, the median household disposable income in the UK was estimated at £31,385. This represents a short-term increase (improvement) from £30,762 in the financial year ending March 2020, and long-term increase (improvement) from £29,237 in the financial year ending March 2016 (Figure 6). All household disposable income estimates are adjusted for inflation and expressed in 2020 to 2021 prices.

Figure 6: In the financial year ending March 2021, median household disposable income has increased (in real terms) compared with the financial year ending March 2020 and the financial year ending March 2016

Median equivalised household disposable income (in 2020 to 2021 prices), UK, financial year ending 1999 to 2000 until financial year ending 2020 to 2021

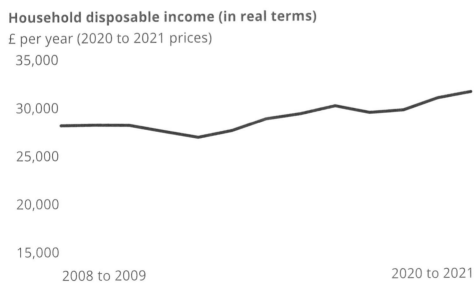

Household disposable income (in real terms)
£ per year (2020 to 2021 prices)

Source: Household Finances Survey - Office for National Statistics

Embed code

Notes:

1. All estimates are adjusted for inflation to 2020 to 2021 prices, using the Consumer Prices Index including owner-occupiers' housing costs (CPIH).

2. The median disposable household income is the estimate for the "middle household" if all households in the UK were sorted in a list by their disposable income.

Download the data

.xlsx (https://www.ons.gov.uk/visualisations/dvc2102/fig6wrapper/datadownload.xlsx)

The percentage of individuals living in households with less than 60% of relative median household income (before housing costs) remained stable over time until March 2021. In April 2020 to March 2021, it was estimated that 15.8% of people in the UK live in low-income households, no change over the long term from 16.4% in April 2015 to March 2016. Please note that the relative low-income data do not account for inflation, so the estimates and change over time may be different in real terms.

The subjective measures of people's financial well-being suggest overall improvement until 2019 to 2020. In 2019 to 2020, prior to the current increases in the cost of living, 44.5% of adults aged 16 years and over in the UK reported being satisfied with the income of their household, a long-term improvement compared with 42.8% in 2014 to 2015. While no change was evident in the percentage of people who find it difficult to manage financially over the same five-year period, it did improve (decrease) by 5.3 percentage points over the decade since 2009 to 2010. In 2019 to 2020, 7.0% of adults aged 16 years and over reported finding it quite or very difficult to manage financially in the UK. However, at present the rising inflation and increasing cost of living are becoming a major source of concern for the public and can be expected to have an impact on people's attitudes and financial well-being in the immediate future. For more information, see our Public opinions and social trends,

Great Britain: 20 to 31 July 2022 bulletin

(https://www.ons.gov.uk/peoplepopulationandcommunity/wellbeing/bulletins/publicopinion

sandsocialtrendsgreatbritain/20to31july2022).

8. Economy

Economy is an important contextual domain for national well-being as it affects the UK's income and wealth, and ability to provide public services. It also more broadly supports jobs, wealth creation and standards of living.

 The commentary in this section is based on annual figures. Monthly and quarterly data are also available on the Office for National Statistics' website.

The coronavirus (COVID-19) pandemic affected the UK's economic well-being by bringing large parts of the economy to a halt and increasing social support spending. At the end of 2021, after almost two years since the beginning of coronavirus, public sector net debt (PSND) reached 97.3% of Gross Domestic Product (GDP). This is the highest value since the early 1960's, and a slight increase on the 95.6% of GDP recorded at the end of 2020. However, the year-on-year increase in PSND as percentage of GDP between 2020 and 2021 (1.7 percentage points) was much lower compared with the increase between 2019 and 2020 (13.2 percentage points).

Net national disposable income per capita, was estimated at £27,023 in 2021. Compared with 2020, this represents a short-term improvement from £24,625, and a long-term improvement from £24,961 in 2016. However, as of 2021 the national disposable income per capita remained below the pre-coronavirus level (£28,125 in 2019).

Figure 7: Net national disposable income per capita has been generally increasing in the UK between 1995 and 2021

Real net national disposable income per head, 2019 chained volume measure, seasonally adjusted, UK, 1995 to 2021

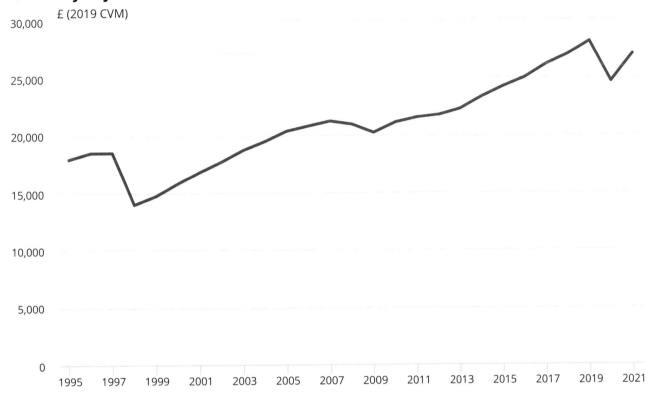

Source: Office for National Statistics – National Accounts

Notes:

1. Net national disposable income per head is a measure of all the national income available to UK residents and institutions after deduction of capital consumption.

2. Estimates are seasonally adjusted and presented at 2019 chained volume measures (CVM).

3. Data are subject to revision as part of the annual National Accounts Blue Book update.

In 2021, the UK's annual average inflation rate, as measured by the Consumer Prices Index including owner occupiers' housing costs (CPIH), was estimated at 2.5%, an increase from 1.0% in 2020.

In June 2022, the inflation rate continued to grow in the UK past the initial economic recovery and reached 8.2%. The effect of rising inflation on the cost of living is now becoming a major source of concern for the public and can be expected to have an impact on national well-being in the immediate future.

9. Education and skills

Education and skills contribute to personal and national well-being by improving individuals' socio-economic outcomes.

In 2020, the estimated value of the UK's human capital, measured as the total net present value of working age adults' projected lifetime earnings in real terms, was £23.8 trillion, an increase (improvement) over both the short term (£23.5 trillion in 2019) and the long term (£23.1 trillion in 2015). The over-time increase in the UK's human capital can be mainly explained by the rise in the number of working-aged people (those aged 16 to 65 years) with at least an undergraduate degree, or equivalent, as their highest level of qualification.

In July to September 2021, 6.8% of adults aged 16 to 64 years were estimated to have no qualifications. This represents a long-term improvement (decrease) from 8.2% in July to September 2016 and is less than half of the percentage reported in July to September 2002 (15.6%).

Figure 8: In July to September 2021, the percentage of working-aged adults with no qualifications was less than half that in July to September 2002

Percentage of adults aged 16 to 64 years with no qualifications, UK, July to September 2002 to July to September 2021

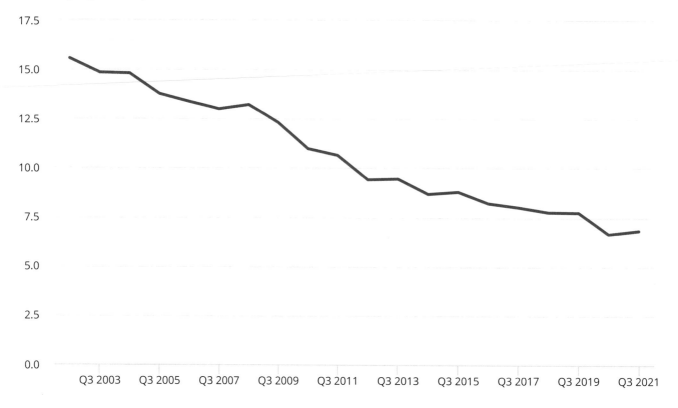

Source: Office for National Statistics – Labour Force Survey

Notes:

1. Estimates for 2002 to 2007 are based on a population of men aged 16 to 64 years and women aged 16 to 59 years. Women aged 60 to 64 years who were in employment are also included.

2. In 2011, the survey question was altered to improve picking up qualifications obtained outside the UK. This has been partly responsible for the drop in percentage of those with no qualifications between 2010 and 2011.

3. Estimates exclude respondents who did not state their qualifications or did not know if they had a qualification.

In January to March 2022, 10.4% of young people aged 16 to 24 years in the UK were Not in Education, Employment or Training (NEET); no change over the previous five years (11.2% in January to March 2017). However, it is an improvement compared with all quarters between January to March 2010 and April to June 2015.

10. Governance

Good governance, underpinned by trust and political engagement of the citizens, contributes to better social and economic outcomes.

In the UK, the percentage of people who tend to trust the national government fluctuated between 2004 and 2022, becoming increasingly volatile since November 2018. In January to February 2022, 22% of adults aged 15 years and over in the UK said that they tend to trust the national government. This is a short-term deterioration (decrease) by 26 percentage points since February to March 2021. In February to March 2021, 48% of adults agreed that they tend to trust the government, the highest percentage recorded since 2004.

Figure 9: Trust in national government has peaked in February to March 2021 and fallen since

Percentage of people who tend to trust the national government, UK, October to November 2004 to January to February 2022

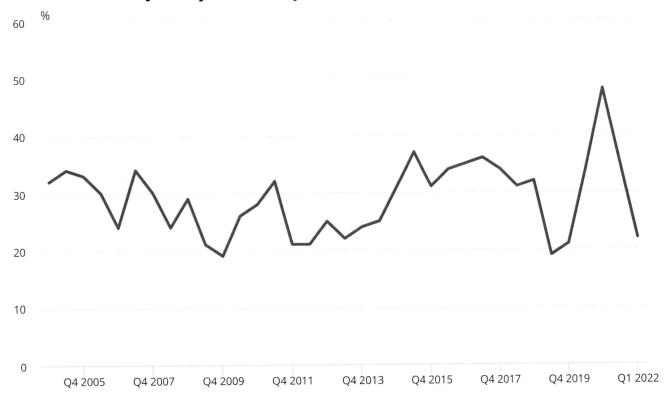

Source: Eurobarometer

Notes:

1. Respondents were asked if they "tend to trust" or "tend not to trust" a range of institutions, including the national government.

For civic engagement, in June to July 2022, 65.8% of adults aged 16 years and over in Great Britain reported feeling that they do not have any say in what the government does.

11. Environment

Natural environment provides services that make human life possible and, as such, can affect people's quality of life.

In March 2021, 40.6 million hectares of the UK's land and sea were designated as protected areas, both a short-term and a long-term improvement compared with 28.6 million hectares in 2019 and 23.5 million hectares in 2016. The percentage of UK energy consumed from renewable sources was 13.6% in 2020, a long-term improvement by 6 percentage points from 7.6% in 2015.

The UK's greenhouse gas emission rates improved (decreased), and almost halved between 1990 and 2020. An estimated 405.5 million tonnes of CO2 equivalent (MtCO2e) greenhouse gas were emitted in the UK in 2020, an improvement over both the short term (447.9 MtCO2e in 2019) and the long term (507.9 MtCO2e in 2015). However, it should be noted that the decrease in greenhouse gas emissions in 2020 was related to the reduction in production and transport in the context of the coronavirus (COVID-19) pandemic. The provisional greenhouse gas emission estimate for 2021 is 424.5 MtCO2e, a short-term deterioration (increase) since 2020 but sustained long-term improvement (decrease) since 483.1 MtCO2e in 2016.

Figure 10: UK greenhouse gas emissions almost halved between 1990 and 2020

Total greenhouse gas emissions, UK, 1990 to 2021

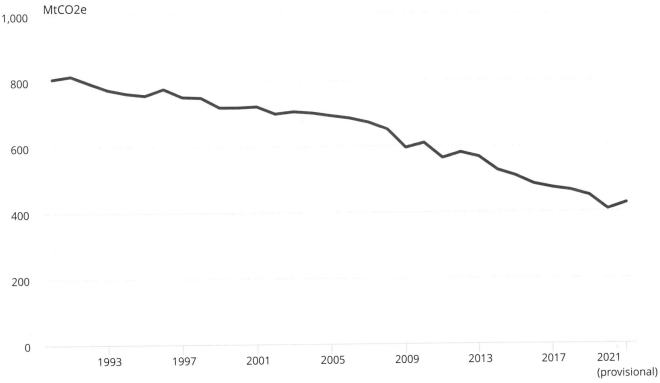

Source: Department for Business, Energy and Industrial Strategy – UK territorial greenhouse gas emissions national statistics

Notes:

1. The 2021 estimate is provisional and subject to revision when the final UK greenhouse gas emission statistics for 2021 will be published.

2. Presented estimates are produced on the basis of UK territory (for example, emissions within the UK territory). The Office for National Statistics also publishes greenhouse gas emission figures that are compiled on the UK resident's basis (for example, include emissions from UK residents abroad and exclude domestic emissions from non-UK residents).

As coronavirus had an impact on reduction in greenhouse gas emissions, the recycling rate for waste from households also decreased. In 2020, 44.4% of household waste was recycled, a small deterioration compared with 46.0% in 2019. Over the long term, no change from 44.5% in 2015 was observed.

12. Future developments

The Measures of National Well-being (MNW) framework was developed by the Office for National Statistics (ONS) in 2011 to monitor and report on "how the UK is doing" by producing indicators on the well-being of the nation through the 10 areas of life people told us mattered most to their well-being.

Reflecting on whether changes to society from the frameworks development to now – including for example changes brought about by the UK's exit from the European Union, the Coronavirus pandemic or the current cost of living challenges, will have affected what matters most to well-being in the UK today; our assessment is that the ten areas of life that were identified as important back in 2011, remain important today. However, at the more detailed level, we want to make sure the 44 measures captured under the framework are still the best measures of well-being in the UK.

In Autumn 2022 we will be launching a consultation to review the existing national well-being measures, to make sure we are still capturing what is most important to the well-being of the UK public today. The consultation will also consider how we should best communicate these well-being insights. If you would like to help inform our review, please let us know via email at qualityoflife@ons.gov.uk. We will launching the consultation at an event (https://measures-of-national-well-being.eventbrite.co.uk) hosted by the National Statistician Sir Ian Diamond on Monday 3rd October – if you are interested in attending, please sign up here.

National well-being constitutes one of the core pillars of the 'Beyond GDP' approach to measuring a nation's progress. As such, this release is being published alongside the latest economic (https://www.ons.gov.uk/economy/grossdomesticproductgdp/bulletins/gdpfirstquarterlyestimateuk/apriltojune2022) and climate change (https://www.ons.gov.uk/economy/environmentalaccounts/articles/climatechangeinsightsuk/august2022) insights to provide a more complete picture of the welfare of the UK and the

UK public. Please see the [blog - Measuring Progress: it's not just about GDP (https://blog.ons.gov.uk/2022/08/12/measuring-progress-gdp-beyond/)](https://blog.ons.gov.uk/2022/08/12/measuring-progress-gdp-beyond/) for more detail on the statistical releases published today."

13. Quality of life in the UK data

Measures of National Well-being Dashboard: Quality of Life in the UK
(https://www.ons.gov.uk/peoplepopulationandcommunity/wellbeing/articles/measureso
fnationalwellbeingdashboardqualityoflifeintheuk/2022-08-12)

Data dashboard | Released 12 August 2022

Data dashboard providing an overview of the UK's progress against 44 indicators across
the 10 domains of national well-being. National level data, trend over time and the
assessment of change are presented for each indicator. The data sources and
associated insight reports for each indicator can be accessed through the dashboard by
following the links in chart subtitles.

Measuring national well-being: domains and measures
(https://www.ons.gov.uk/peoplepopulationandcommunity/wellbeing/datasets/measurin
gnationalwellbeingdomainsandmeasures)

Dataset | Released 12 August 2022

Latest data, times series data and detailed information for the measures of national
well-being. Includes estimates for all indicators from each domain, sub-national
breakdowns (where available), and links to the data sources and associated release.

Quarterly personal well-being estimates – seasonally adjusted
(https://www.ons.gov.uk/peoplepopulationandcommunity/wellbeing/datasets/quarterly
personalwellbeingestimatesseasonallyadjusted)

Dataset | Released on 12 August 2022

Seasonally adjusted quarterly estimates of life satisfaction, feeling that the things done
in life are worthwhile, happiness and anxiety in the UK.

Quality of information for quarterly personal well-being estimates
(https://www.ons.gov.uk/peoplepopulationandcommunity/wellbeing/datasets/qualityofi
nformationforquarterlypersonalwellbeingestimates)
Dataset | Released on 12 August 2022
Confidence intervals and sample sizes for quarterly estimates of personal well-being in
the UK.

Quarterly personal well-being estimates – non-seasonally adjusted
(https://www.ons.gov.uk/peoplepopulationandcommunity/wellbeing/datasets/quarterly
personalwellbeingestimatesnonseasonallyadjusted)
Dataset | Released on 12 August 2022
Non-seasonally adjusted quarterly estimates of life satisfaction, feeling that the things
done in life are worthwhile, happiness and anxiety in the UK.

14. Glossary

Measures of national well-being

There are ten domains of national well-being that the UK public told us were the areas of life that mattered most to them:

- personal well-being

- our relationships

- health

- what we do

- where we live

- personal finance

- economy

- education and skills

- governance

- environment

Within these ten domains there are 44 indicators of national well-being. The indicators include both objective measures (for example, unemployment rate) and subjective measures (for example, job satisfaction) to provide a comprehensive picture of the nation's well-being and societal progress.

Personal well-being

In the UK, personal well-being has been measured since April 2011 using questions on:

- life satisfaction

- whether we think the things we do in life are worthwhile

- happiness

- anxiety

For more information, see the Personal well-being user guidance
(https://www.ons.gov.uk/peoplepopulationandcommunity/wellbeing/methodologies/person
alwellbeingsurveyuserguide).

Social capital

Social capital is a term used to describe the extent and nature of our connections with
others and the collective attitudes and behaviours between people that support a well-
functioning, close-knit society.

It is measured through the four core domains of:

- personal relationships

- social network support

- civic engagement

- trust and cooperative norms

For more information on measuring social capital, see the Social capital in the UK: April 2020
to March 2021 bulletin
(https://www.ons.gov.uk/peoplepopulationandcommunity/wellbeing/bulletins/socialcapitali
ntheuk/latest).

15. Measuring the data

National well-being indicators

This release provides an update on 44 indicators across 10 domains of national well-being, using the latest data available as of July 2022. The selection of indicators is based on the national well-being framework established by the Office for National Statistics (ONS) in 2011, following a public consultation. Some changes to the data sources and specific indicators used, compared with previous releases, were necessary for this update to ensure data availability and comparability. We have updated three existing indicators and added three new ones to reflect the Government Statistical Service (GSS) social capital harmonised standard and improve measurement of social capital as part of national well-being.

We have only commented on the indicators where the latest estimate is available for 2019 to 2020 or later periods. For the majority, only the national level data are discussed. Any potential sub-population inequalities in the data are not captured.

The full set of national well-being estimates, including historical data and assessment of over-time change where possible, and the full list of indicator changes are available in the accompanying data tables. The sub-population breakdowns by country and the International Territorial Level 1 (ITL1) region, age and sex are also provided where possible.

All analysed data were known to be current as of 28 July 2022. Data sources for individual indicators can be accessed by following source links in our National well-being dashboard and our Quality of life data tables.

Data coverage

The data come from several data sources that differ in terms of covered geographies, sampled populations and periods of data collection. They are referenced throughout for each indicator and detailed in the accompanying datasets.

In 2020 and 2021, several of the data sources were affected by the coronavirus (COVID-19) pandemic in terms of the mode and timeliness of data collection or sample composition. Therefore, caution should be taken when making comparisons between indicators and over-time.

For the indicators where the UK-wide data are not available, alternative data sources may exist for Wales, Scotland and Northern Ireland, but differences in methodology may affect comparability of the data. For national well-being data collected by the devolved administrations, see the Related links section.

Comparability

Short-term change is assessed by comparison to the previous year, or the latest previous figure if one year comparison is not available. Long-term change is defined as change over the previous five years or, if not available, the next previous figure.

Confidence intervals are provided within the data tables alongside this release (where available). Where changes over time are presented in this bulletin, associated confidence intervals are used to assess the statistical significance of the differences.

For some of the indicators that are not based on survey data, confidence intervals are not available. In those cases, change over time has not been assessed or has been assessed based on guidance from the data owner. When interpreting the latest estimates and the presented assessments of change, the potential impact of the coronavirus pandemic on individual's attitudes and survey responses, as well as the impact on data collection, should be kept in mind, given the major disruption COVID-19 caused in people's lives.

As most of the data comes from self-completion household surveys, the estimates may not be representative for individuals who do not live in private residential households.

Feedback

In autumn 2022 we will be launching a consultation to review the existing national well-being measures and data communication tools. If you would like to help inform our review, please let us know via email at qualityoflife@ons.gov.uk. If you are interested in attending our online launch event, please sign up via Eventbrite (https://measures-of-national-well-being.eventbrite.co.uk).

16. Strengths and limitations

Personal well-being data presented for the periods Quarter 1 (Jan to Mar) 2020 to Quarter 2 (Apr to June) 2021, sourced from the Annual Population Survey datasets year ending March 2020 to year ending June 2021, are affected by an error in the calculation of population weights. This affects the age breakdown of the population in Wales to a small extent. Breakdowns for the UK as a whole would be largely unaffected. We aim to explore the extent of this error on personal well-being estimates and revise them as necessary in September 2022.

Comparisons over time and between indicators must be made with caution as the estimates come from several data sources with different geographical coverage and data collection periods (for more information see datasets (https://www.ons.gov.uk/peoplepopulationandcommunity/wellbeing/bulletins/qualityoflifein theuk/august2022/relateddata)).

Data availability limits the timeliness of some of the insights, and so the effect of more recent socio-economic events (for example, the rising cost of living) on national well-being cannot be evaluated in this release.

The majority of the indicators are based on cross-sectional survey data. Information was collected from a sample of the population of interest at a point in time, and then weighted to adjust the estimates for representativeness of the population. Therefore, the estimates are subject to uncertainty, which is expressed using 95% confidence intervals (where available). This is a conservative method of assessing change, so it is possible that significant differences exist in the data that have not been identified using this method. The ONS guidance on uncertainty (https://www.ons.gov.uk/methodology/methodologytopicsandstatisticalconcepts/uncertaint yandhowwemeasureit) contains more information on how we measure and communicate uncertainty for survey data.

All analysis has been done on unrounded figures. Some figures may not sum because of rounding.

For the indicators where the UK-wide data are not available, alternative data sources may exist for the devolved administrations (Wales, Scotland and Northern Ireland), but differences in methodology affect comparability of the data. For national well-being data collected by the devolved administrations, see the Scottish Government's National Indicator Performance (https://nationalperformance.gov.scot/measuring-progress/national-indicator-performance), the Welsh Government's Wellbeing of Wales: national indicators (https://gov.wales/wellbeing-wales-national-indicators) and Wellbeing of Wales releases (https://gov.wales/wellbeing-wales), and the Northern Ireland Statistics and Research Agency's Wellbeing in Northern Ireland (https://www.nisra.gov.uk/statistics/people-places-and-culture/wellbeing-northern-ireland).

17. Related links

GDP quarterly national accounts, UK: April to June 2022
(https://www.ons.gov.uk/economy/grossdomesticproductgdp/bulletins/gdpfirstquarterl ypfirstquaute/
apriltojune2022)

Bulletin | Released 12 August 2022

Revised quarterly estimate of gross domestic product (GDP) for the UK. Uses additional data to provide a more precise indication of economic growth than the first estimate.

Climate Change Insights, UK: August 2022
(https://www.ons.gov.uk/economy/environmentalaccounts/articles/
climatechangeinsigh

Bulletin | Released 12 August 2022

Quarterly publication bringing together the latest climate change-related statistics and analysis from a range of sources.

Contact details for this statistical bulletin

Ida Sadlowska and Eleanor Rees
qualityoflife@ons.gov.uk
Telephone: +44 300 0671543

Statistical bulletin

Trust in government, UK: 2022

Trust in government and institutions, opinions of public services and attitudes toward political issues. UK-specific results. Experimental Statistics.

Contact:
Matthew Lelii
publicservicesanalysis@ons.gov.uk
+44 1633 456921

Release date:
13 July 2022

Next release:
To be announced

Table of contents

1 . Main points

- 35% of the UK population stated that they trusted the national government, which is lower than the Organisation for Economic Co-operation and Development (OECD) average (41%).

- 42% of the population reported that they trusted local government and 55% trusted the Civil Service.

- Trust in public services was higher than trust in the national or local governments, with the NHS the most trusted public service (80%), followed by the courts and legal system (68%).

- 75% of the population believed that the UK government should place a higher priority on creating conditions for businesses to thrive, 64% said they should place higher priority on reducing climate change and 54% believe they should place higher priority on reducing the national debt.

2 . Trust in government

The UK Trust in Government Survey is a part of an international study commissioned and coordinated by the Organisation for Economic Co-operation and Development (OECD). The survey looks at people's trust in governments and institutions, opinions about public services and attitudes towards political issues. The Cabinet Office asked the Office for National Statistics (ONS) to undertake the survey on behalf of the UK and the fieldwork took place in March 2022. This bulletin focuses on the results of the UK survey, which included all the OECD survey questions and additional UK-focussed questions. The OECD have published their own report, which looks at the results across all participating countries.

Three-quarters (75%) of the UK population reported that they are trusting of most other people, higher than the average among the OECD countries who participated in the survey (67%). One-third (35%) of the UK population reported that they trust their national government, lower than the average across the OECD countries (41%). Half (49%) of the UK population said they did not trust the national government. UK respondents were asked specifically about their trust in the UK Government rather than any of the devolved Governments in Scotland, Wales or Northern Ireland.

Figure 1: UK people are more trusting of other people than of the government, relative to other OECD countries

International comparison of the levels of trust in people and governments, OECD countries, 2021 to 2022

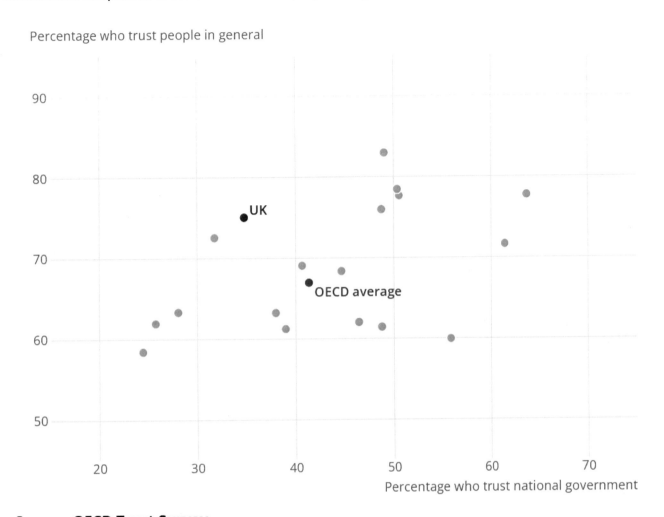

Source: OECD Trust Survey

Notes:

1. Levels of trust were reported on a 0 to 10 scale, where 0 is "not at all" and 10 is "completely".

2. The "trust" category represents scores of 6 to 10.

3. To see the results for each of the participating countries in the OECD trust survey, please see the OECD report.

Download the data

.xlsx

Levels of trust in political and administrative institutions varied (Figure 2). Only one in five (20%) of the UK population reported trust in the political parties, while more than half (55%) reported that they trust the Civil Service.

Figure 2: Levels of trust in government varied by type of institution

Levels of trust, UK, March 2022

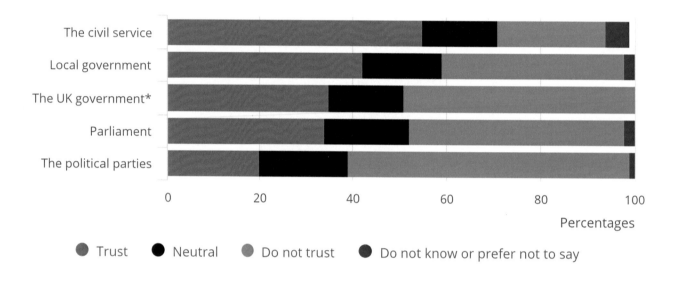

Figure 2: Levels of trust in government varied by type of institution

Levels of trust, UK, March 2022

Source: Office for National Statistics - Trust in Government Survey, March 2022

Notes:

1. Levels of trust were reported on a 0 to 10 scale, where 0 is "not at all" and 10 is "completely".

2. The "trust" category represents scores of 6 to 10, "neutral" represents scores of 5 and "do not trust" represents scores of 0 to 4.

3. The category "Do not know or prefer not to say" for the UK government is based on a sample size of less than 30, so should be treated with caution. This is marked with an asterisk (*).

4. Values may not add to 100% owing to rounding.

Drivers of trust

The OECD has identified five drivers that can influence trust: integrity, responsiveness, reliability, openness, and fairness. Three questions were asked for each of the five drivers, where respondents were asked how likely they thought it was that scenarios based on these drivers of trust would happen in the UK. The full results of these questions can be found in our accompanying dataset. Some of the questions, which show larger differences between the UK results and the OECD averages, are referenced below.

Openness

The majority of the UK population (78%) thought it was likely that they would easily find information about administrative procedures (for example, obtaining a passport or applying for benefits), higher than the OECD average of 65%.

Additionally, half of the UK population (50%) felt it was likely that they would have an opportunity to voice their views if a decision affecting the community were to be made by the local government, higher than the OECD average of 41%.

Fairness

More than two-thirds (68%) felt it was likely that their application for a benefit or service would be treated fairly, compared with the OECD average of 59%.

Reliability

Just over half (57%) of the UK population thought it was likely that government institutions would be prepared to protect people's lives if a new serious contagious disease spreads, compared with the OECD average of 49%. To note, this survey took place in March 2022, two years after the first lockdowns were implemented in the UK in response to the coronavirus (COVID-19) pandemic.

Responsiveness

Less than one-third (30%) of the UK population thought it was likely that a national policy would be changed if the majority of people expressed a view against it, lower than the OECD average of 36%. Half (51%) of the UK population thought a change was unlikely, compared with an OECD average of 40%.

Around one-third (34%) felt it was likely that a public service that was working badly would be improved if many people complained, lower than the OECD average (40%). Around half (49%) thought it was unlikely the service would be improved, compared with an OECD average of 38%.

Integrity

One-quarter (25%) of the UK population thought that a high-level politician would likely refuse a well-paid job in the private sector in exchange for granting a political favour, lower than the OECD average of 30%. Nearly two-thirds (62%) thought it was unlikely they would refuse, compared with an OECD average of 48%.

Associations between trust and drivers of trust

This section explores how the responses to the drivers of trust scenarios (as explained above) are associated with the overall level of trust in the UK government and the Civil Service. In particular, the scenario which has the largest variation in mean trust score when comparing responses that said a scenario was likely or unlikely, has been identified. See Section 7: Measuring the data for more information on how mean scores were calculated.

UK government

Of all fifteen scenarios, differences in opinion about the reliability of business conditions resulted in the largest variation in trust scores for the UK government. Of those who thought it likely that business conditions government can influence would be stable and predictable, the mean trust score for the UK government was 5.5 out of 10. Of those who thought that stability and predictability was unlikely, the mean score was 2.5.

Civil Service

Differences in opinion about the responsiveness of public services had the largest variation in trust scores for the Civil Service. Of those who thought it likely that a public agency would adopt an innovative idea that could improve a public service, the mean trust score for the Civil Service was 6.7 out of 10. Of those who thought it unlikely, the mean score was 4.7.

3 . Public services

As part of the UK Trust in Government study, additional questions were asked regarding public services, which were not explored in the Organisation for Economic Co-operation and Development (OECD) study. As a result, in the following sections comparisons between the UK and the OECD average are not always available. The scope of each public service is defined within the data reference tables.

Use of public services

The majority (80%) of the UK population reported that they had used the NHS themselves in the last 12 months. Smaller proportions had accessed other public services; the police (11%), education (14%) and social services (3%). Nearly one-third (29%) reported that either they or their child had been enrolled in an educational institution in the last two years.

Trust and satisfaction with public services

Respondents were asked separately about their trust and satisfaction in each public service. Levels of trust in public services were higher than those for government and political institutions (see Section 2: Trust in government). The public service with the highest level of trust was the NHS (80%), followed by the courts and legal system (68%).

Figure 3: High levels of trust were reported for the NHS

Levels of trust in public institutions, UK, March 2022

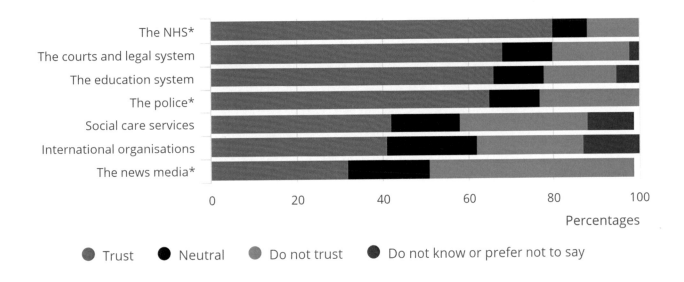

Figure 3: High levels of trust were reported for the NHS

Levels of trust in public institutions, UK, March 2022

Source: Office for National Statistics - Trust in Government Survey, March 2022

Notes:

1. Levels of trust were reported on a 0 to 10 scale, where 0 is "not at all" and 10 is "completely".

2. The "trust" category represents scores of 6 to 10, "neutral" represents scores of 5 and "do not trust" represents scores of 0 to 4.

3. For the NHS, the police and the news media, the category "Do not know or prefer not to say" is based on a sample size of less than 30, so should be treated with caution. These are marked with an asterisk (*).

4. Values may not add to 100% owing to rounding.

More than half of the UK population were satisfied with the country's public services, with the exception of social care services. More than two-thirds (69%) reported being satisfied with the NHS (the public service with the highest satisfaction score), higher than the OECD average for their respective health services (62%).

Figure 4: High levels of satisfaction were reported for the NHS

Levels of satisfaction in public institutions, UK, March 2022

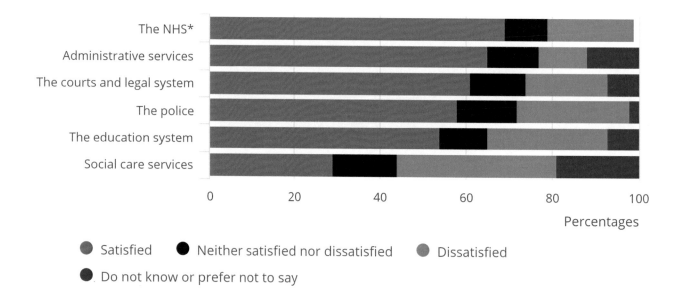

Figure 4: High levels of satisfaction were reported for the NHS

Levels of satisfaction in public institutions, UK, March 2022

Source: Office for National Statistics - Trust in Government Survey, March 2022

Notes:

1. Levels of satisfaction were reported on a 0 to 10 scale, where 0 is "not at all satisfied" and 10 is "completely satisfied".

2. The "satisfied" category represents scores of 6 to 10, "neutral" represents scores of 5 and "dissatisfied" represents scores of 0 to 4.

3. The category "Do not know or prefer not to say" for the NHS is based on a sample size of less than 30, so should be treated with caution. This is marked with an asterisk (*).

4. Values may not add to 100% owing to rounding.

Trust in public institutions was associated with the level of satisfaction in those institutions (Figure 5). The police saw the largest variation in trust scores between those who were satisfied and dissatisfied with the service. Of those who reported that they were satisfied with the police in the UK, the average trust score for the police was 7.4. Of those who were dissatisfied with the police, the average score was 3.5. See Section 7: Measuring the data for more information on how mean scores were calculated.

Figure 5: High levels of trust were associated with high levels of satisfaction with public services

Trust scores for people satisfied and dissatisfied with public services, UK, March 2022

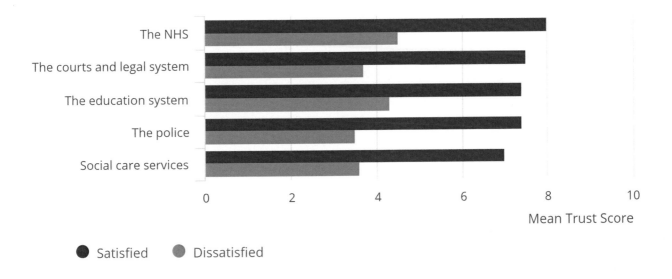

Figure 5: High levels of trust were associated with high levels of satisfaction with public services

Trust scores for people satisfied and dissatisfied with public services, UK, March 2022

Source: Office for National Statistics - Trust in Government Survey, March 2022

Notes:

1. Levels of trust and satisfaction were reported on a 0 to 10 scale, where 0 is "not at all" and 10 is "completely".

2. The "satisfied" category represents satisfaction scores of 6 to 10 and "dissatisfied" represents satisfaction scores of 0 to 4.

4 . Political participation and attitudes

Political participation

Half (49%) of the UK population felt confident in their ability to participate in politics, higher than the Organisation for Economic Co-operation and Development (OECD) average (41%). The majority (82%) of people had participated in at least one political activity in the last 12 months. On average, respondents had participated in two political activities. Most people reported signing a petition (57%) or voting in the last local election (56%).

The majority (58%) of the population were not confident that people like them have a say in what the UK government does. Over one-third (36%) were not confident in their own ability to participate in politics.

Table 1: Political activities in the last 12 months, UK, March 2022

	Percentage reporting participation
Signed a petition, including an e-mail or online petition	57
Voted in last local or municipal election (if there were any)	56
Boycotted certain products for political reasons	27
Contacted a politician, government or local government official	22
Provided input or feedback on government policy, law or document	18
Posted or forwarded political content on social media	18
Worn or displayed a campaign badge or sticker	7
Attended a meeting of a trade union, political party or political action group	5
Taken part in a public demonstration	4
Participated in a Citizen Assembly, Citizen Dialogue or Citizen Jury*	1
None of these	18

Source: Office for National Statistics - Trust in Government Survey, March 2022

Notes

1. The category "Participated in a Citizen Assembly, Citizen Dialogue or Citizen Jury" is based on a sample size of less than 30, so should be treated with caution. This is marked with an asterisk (*).

2. Respondents were able to select more than one option. Therefore, percentages will not sum to 100%.

Long-term policies and global challenges

Most of the UK population felt that the UK government should prioritise businesses and workers more (Figure 6). Three-quarters (75%) wanted more priority placed upon creating conditions for businesses to thrive. Around two-thirds thought that helping workers adapt to new technologies and providing equal opportunities for all should be prioritised (66% and 64%, respectively).

While two-thirds (64%) of the UK population felt that reducing the UK's contribution to climate change should be more of a priority of the government, one in ten (11%) said it should be less of a priority for the UK government.

Figure 6: People favoured more priority given to creating favourable business conditions and helping workers

Issues the UK government should prioritise more, about the same, or less, UK, March 2022

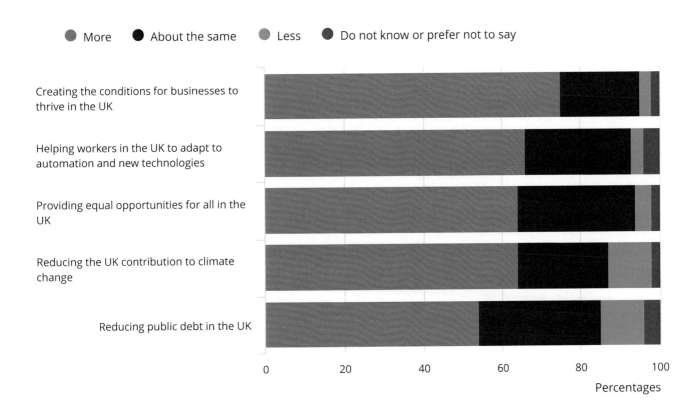

Source: Office for National Statistics - Trust in Government Survey, March 2022

Two-thirds (66%) felt that the UK government should prioritise joining forces with other governments internationally to better tackle global challenges. The majority (75%) chose climate change as one of the top three issues they believe is best addressed by working with other countries rather than by the UK alone. A minority (16%) agree that existing international agreements are sufficient to solve long-term issues facing humanity (such as migration and climate change) and around one-quarter (27%) were not at all confident that the UK will succeed in reducing greenhouse gas emissions in the next 10 years.

5 . Data

Trust in Government UK data
Dataset | Released 13 July 2022
Indicators from the Trust in Government Survey to monitor people's trust across different institutions and levels of government. The dataset includes data on drivers of trust, political attitudes, political participation and satisfaction with public services.

Organisation for Economic Co-operation and Development (OECD) Trust in Government
OECD study | Released 13 July 2022
The OECD have published a report covering the international results of the study. Data are available through their data portal.

6 . Glossary

Civil Service

Non-elected government employees at central or local levels of government.

Climate change

Climate change is the long-term shift in average weather patterns across the world. Since the mid-1800s, humans have contributed to the release of carbon dioxide and other greenhouse gases into the air. This causes global temperatures to rise, resulting in long-term changes to the climate.

UK Government

The UK government consists of the Prime Minister, their Cabinet and junior ministers, supported by the teams of non-political civil servants that work in government departments.

7 . Measuring the data

This release contains data from the Trust in Government survey. The survey was undertaken by the Office for National Statistics (ONS) on behalf of the Cabinet Office and the Organisation for Economic Co-operation and Development (OECD).

The survey was completed online between 11 and 27 March 2022. In a small number of cases (less than 0.2%) the respondent completed the survey over the telephone with an ONS Telephone Operator.

Sampling and weighting

A total of 4,071 adults (aged 18 years or over) living in the UK were sampled and invited to complete the survey. These were selected from those who had previously completed the Opinions and Lifestyle Survey (those living in Great Britain) or the European Health Interview Survey (those living in Northern Ireland). The responding sample was 3,162 individuals, representing a 78% response rate.

Survey weights were applied to make estimates representative of the population.

More quality and methodology information on strengths and limitations, appropriate uses and how the data were created is available in our accompanying Trust in Government Quality and Methodology Information (QMI).

Uncertainty

View more information on how we measure and communicate uncertainty for our surveys.

Experimental Statistics

Data in this release are Experimental Statistics. The data collection methodology used is new and is therefore subject to further evaluation and modification.

Average trust and satisfaction scores

Trust and satisfaction questions are answered on a scale of 0 to 10, with 0 being "not at all" and 10 being "completely". There is also an option for respondents to answer, "don't know" and on some questions, "prefer not to say". Average trust and satisfaction scores represent the mean score for all respondents who gave an answer between 0 and 10. This is the sum of all scores, divided by the number of respondents.

8 . Related links

Organisation for Economic Co-operation and Development (OECD) Trust in Government
OECD study | Released 13 July 2022
The report and methodology of the wider international study of OECD countries on Trust in Government.

Trust in Government Survey QMI
Methodology | Released 13 July 2022
Quality and Methodology Information (QMI) for the Trust in Government Survey, detailing strengths and limitations of the data, methods used, and data uses and users.

Coronavirus and contributors to subnational well-being: January to March 2021

Regression analysis of the Opinions and Lifestyle Survey to provide insight into the impact of the coronavirus (COVID-19) pandemic, to better understand which socio-demographic and economic factors were most associated with levels of happiness in England and Wales in early 2021.

Contact:

Will Haste

Release date:

26 May 2021

Next release:

To be announced

Table of contents

1. Main points

- Over the past year, average happiness for England and Wales was lower than the pre-pandemic (February 2020) average of 7.2; London recorded lower average happiness than rural areas or other urban areas, dropping to a low of 6.5 in early 2021.

- Reported loneliness was found to have the strongest association to happiness of any other factor considered; lonely adults were likely to report lower happiness scores than less lonely adults, with London having the largest proportion of adults who felt lonely at least some of the time (29%).

- Adults in urban areas (including London) who had worked from home over the last seven days were more likely to report lower levels of happiness than those who had not worked from home.

- When compared with the baseline of respondents aged 75 years or over, all younger adults across all areas had significantly lower levels of happiness; this indicates that people over the age of 75 years are most likely to report the highest level of happiness, especially compared with those aged 35 to 44 years.

2. Understanding the impact on society

This bulletin contains data and indicators from the Office for National Statistics' (ONS') Opinions and Lifestyle Survey (OPN) to understand the impact of the coronavirus (COVID-19) pandemic. The pandemic has led to personal happiness becoming a headline issue and, in this analysis, we present information to help understand the factors currently affecting changes in well-being.

This bulletin presents the results of regression analysis to show the impact of different demographic, economic and behavioural factors on happiness levels in England and Wales. Of the available metrics, happiness was chosen because it is a short-term metric with the question framed as "how happy did you feel yesterday?". This allows us to focus specifically on how people's well-being was affected within the time period, and adds to existing analysis already conducted on Coronavirus and anxiety (https://www.ons.gov.uk/peoplepopulationandcommunity/wellbeing/articles/coronavirusan danxietygreatbritain/3april2020to10may2020).

Results are presented for rural areas, urban areas, and London, to analyse these types of geography separately. The 2011 rural/urban classification (https://www.ons.gov.uk/methodology/geography/geographicalproducts/ruralurbanclassific ations/2011ruralurbanclassification) defines whether a census output area was urban if it belongs to a built-up area with more than 10,000 inhabitants, otherwise the area is defined as rural. Scottish data have been excluded from the analysis because of differing definitions between Scotland and the rest of Great Britain.

Regression analysis is used to examine associations between personal well-being and individual characteristics and circumstances. This technique can identify the strength and direction of these relationships, but it cannot conclude that one factor causes another. The data used for the regression analysis covers the period 7 January 2021 to 28 March 2021, referred to as "early 2021".

The OPN includes questions on COVID-19 specific behaviours and attitudes, which allows us to build a more relevant model on how the pandemic has affected personal well-being. Well-being regression analysis by the ONS is typically done using the Annual Population Survey (APS) using a particular modelling approach. The results presented here are using a different data source and different modelling approach so users should exercise caution in drawing direct comparisons between these results and previous publications. The article Data collection changes due to the pandemic and their impact on estimating personal well-being (https://www.ons.gov.uk/peoplepopulationandcommunity/wellbeing/methodologies/datacollectionchangesduetothepandemicandtheirimpactonestimatingpersonalwellbeing) provides further information on differences between OPN and APS estimates.

For further explanation of the approach taken and how to interpret our findings, see the methodology section in Measuring the data (https://publishing.ons.gov.uk/peoplepopulationandcommunity/wellbeing/bulletins/coronavirusandcontributorstosubnationalwellbeing/januarytomarch2021#measuring-the-data).

3. Average happiness throughout the pandemic

According to responses to the Opinions and Lifestyle Survey (OPN), average happiness for England and Wales in all periods analysed was lower than the pre-coronavirus (COVID-19) pandemic average of 7.2 (https://www.ons.gov.uk/peoplepopulationandcommunity/healthandsocialcare/healthandwellbeing/bulletins/coronavirusandthesocialimpactsongreatbritain/16april2021) measured in February 2020.

Figure 1: Average happiness was higher in rural areas than in urban areas or London in all periods, March 2020 to March 2021

Rural and urban areas, England and Wales 20 March 2020 to 28 March 2021

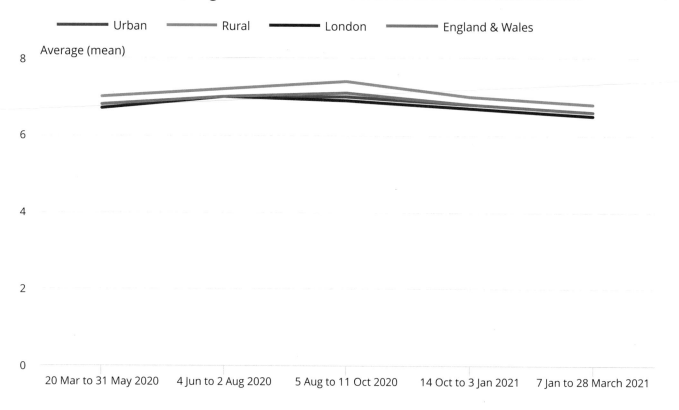

Source: Office for National Statistics – Opinions and Lifestyle Survey

Notes:

1. Question asked: "How happy did you feel yesterday where 0 is not at all happy and 10 is completely happy?"

2. Cases in which respondents did not answer the question have been excluded from the analysis.

3. Confidence intervals are provided in the datasets associated with this bulletin. As a general rule, if the confidence interval around one estimate overlaps with the interval around another, we cannot say with certainty that there is more than a chance difference between the two estimates.

4. The 2011 rural/urban classification was used to create the rural and urban breakdowns. More information on this can be found here: 2011 rural/urban classification - Office for National Statistics

(https://www.ons.gov.uk/methodology/geography/geographicalproducts/ruralurbanclas sifications/2011ruralurbanclassification).

Over the past year, average happiness was highest in rural areas, peaking in autumn 2020 at 7.4 out of 10. Adults living in London reported the lowest level of happiness in every period, compared with urban areas and rural areas in the rest of the country, with London reaching its lowest level (6.5) in early 2021. Happiness levels in urban areas were similar to the England and Wales national average across all periods analysed, with no variation greater than 0.1 in average happiness. This is driven by the fact that the majority of adults were living in urban areas in early 2021 (65%), compared with rural areas (20%) and London (15%).

4. Factors affecting happiness in London, rural and urban areas

The five factors most strongly associated with happiness across all areas analysed included:

- how lonely a respondent feels (this variable showed the strongest correlation with happiness)

- ability to save money over the next 12 months

- age group

- how much people feel that they have enough information to protect themselves from the coronavirus (COVID-19) pandemic

- level of comfort in leaving home

Behavioural characteristics

Figure 2: How often a person reported feeling lonely was associated to the biggest change in happiness of any factor

Rural and urban areas, 7 January to 28 March 2021

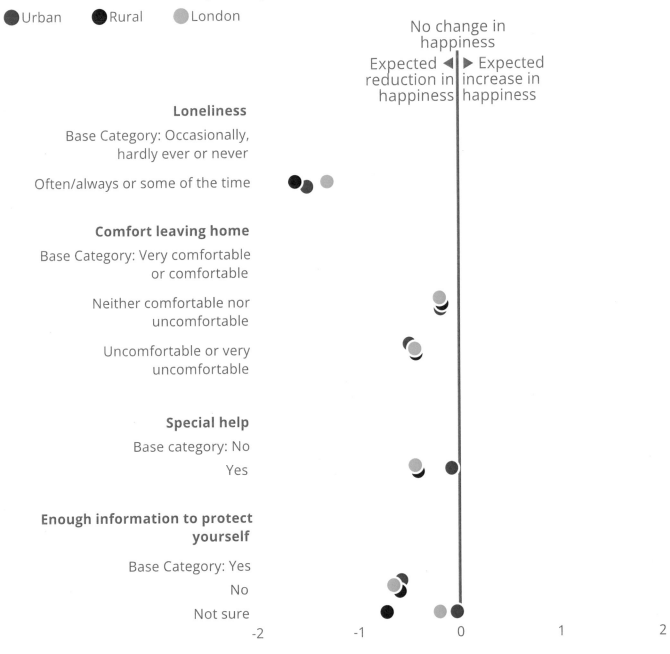

Source: **Office for National Statistics – Opinions and Lifestyle Survey**

Download the data

(https://www.ons.gov.uk/visualisations/dvc1304/behaviour/datadownload.xlsx)

Notes

1. Question: "And how often do you feel lonely?"

2. Question: "At this time, how comfortable or uncomfortable do you feel about leaving your home due to the coronavirus (COVID-19) pandemic?"

3. Question: "Is there anyone living with you who is sick, disabled, or over 70 whom you look after or give special help to?"

4. Question: "Do you feel like you have enough information about how to protect yourself from the Coronavirus (COVID-19)?"

5. The 2011 Rural/Urban classification was used to create the rural and urban classes, more information on this can be found here: 2011 rural/urban classification - Office for National Statistics (https://www.ons.gov.uk/methodology/geography/geographicalproducts/ruralurbanclassifications/2011ruralurbanclassification).

6. The results shown in Figure 2 are statistically significant at the 5% level unless mentioned.

Loneliness

A respondent who reported feeling lonely often, always or some of the time, was found to have the strongest association to happiness of any factor considered in these models, as was the case in analysis of well-being during the first lockdown in 2020. (https://www.ons.gov.uk/peoplepopulationandcommunity/wellbeing/articles/coronavirusandanxietygreatbritain/3april2020to10may2020) The model found that adults feeling lonely at least some of the time can affect their happiness score by around double the impact of any other behavioural factor analysed.

Holding all other factors constant, loneliness had the greatest impact on levels of happiness of adults in rural areas. This would have affected the 24% of adults in rural areas who responded to the survey saying they felt lonely at least some of the time. Although the effect of loneliness in urban areas and London was estimated to be slightly lower (affecting happiness by negative 1.5 points and negative 1.3 points respectively compared with rural areas where loneliness affected happiness levels by negative 1.6 points), a higher percentage of adults in urban areas (27%) and London (29%) reported feeling lonely.

This may be partly explained by demographic differences, as recent research showed that 16- to 29-year-olds were the most likely age group to report feeling lonely during lockdowns (https://www.ons.gov.uk/peoplepopulationandcommunity/wellbeing/articles/mappingloneli nessduringthecoronaviruspandemic/2021-04-07), and urban areas had slightly younger demographic profiles than rural areas.

Comfort leaving home

In all areas, respondents who were uncomfortable leaving home (because of the coronavirus pandemic) were strongly associated with lower levels of happiness when compared with those who were comfortable leaving home. This association was strongest in urban areas, and the percentage of people who felt uncomfortable leaving home was broadly similar across the areas analysed, with all values falling in the range of 37% to 40%.

Providing special help

In all areas, living with someone who was sick, disabled, or over 70 years old to whom the respondent gives special help, was associated with lower levels of happiness compared with those who did not. The biggest difference in expected happiness was seen in London but this area had the lowest proportion of adults who reported providing special help: 6% compared with rural and urban areas (8% and 9% respectively). Compared with the average for England and Wales, a lower percentage of London residents reported having a disability (17% compared with 23%), which likely drives the lower proportion of carers.

Enough information

People who felt they did not have enough information to protect themselves from the pandemic were associated with lower levels of happiness than those who answered that they did. Overall, a low percentage of adults in England and Wales did not feel they had enough information to protect themselves (3%) with the highest proportion found in London (4%).

Work and financial variables

Figure 3: Adults in London and urban areas who had worked from home over the last 7 days were likely to report lower levels of happiness than those who had not worked from home

Rural and urban areas, 7 January to 28 March 2021

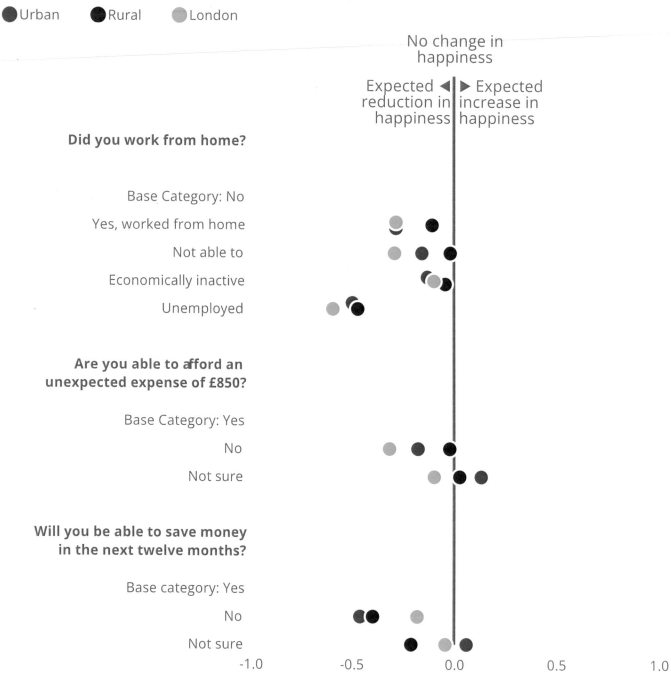

Source: Office for National Statistics – Opinions and Lifestyle Survey

Embed code

Source: Office for National Statistics – Opinions and Lifestyle Survey

Download the data

(https://www.ons.gov.uk/visualisations/dvc1304/work/datadownload.xlsx)

Notes

1. Question: "In the past seven days, have you worked from home because of the Coronavirus (COVID-19) pandemic?"

2. Question: "Could your household afford to pay an unexpected, but necessary, expense of £850?"

3. Question: "In view of the general economic situation, do you think you will be able to save any money in the next twelve months?"

4. For this survey, a person is said to be working if last week: they had a paid job, either as an employee or self-employed; or they did any casual work for payment; or they did any unpaid or voluntary work.

5. The definitions of employment, unemployment, and economic inactivity are based upon International Labour Organisation (ILO) definitions. Further information about labour market definitions can be found at: A guide to labour market statistics - Office for National Statistics (https://www.ons.gov.uk/employmentandlabourmarket/peopleinwork/employmentand employeetypes/methodologies/aguidetolabourmarketstatistics).

6. The 2011 Rural/Urban classification was used to create the rural and urban classes, more information on this can be found here: 2011 rural/urban classification - Office for National Statistics (https://www.ons.gov.uk/methodology/geography/geographicalproducts/ruralurbanclas sifications/2011ruralurbanclassification).

7. The results shown in Figure 3 are statistically significant at the 5% level unless mentioned.

Working status

Compared with the reference group of workers who did not work from home, adults who worked from home over the seven days before responding to the survey reported lower happiness in urban areas and London, but there was no significant trend in rural areas. As the ability of someone to work from home is linked to the occupation they work in, this trend may indicate that people who work in occupations where they have the option not to work from home may be happier.

Respondents who were unable to work from home were more likely to report lower levels of happiness in urban areas and London, but not in rural areas. Overall, these results indicate that whether someone works from home or not does have an impact on people's happiness in urban areas, but not in rural areas.

Unemployed respondents reported lower levels of happiness than employed respondents. The effect was slightly more pronounced in London and urban areas than in rural areas.

Financial variables

Adults living in households that reported they would be unable to afford an unexpected, but necessary, payment of £850 were likely to report lower levels of happiness in urban areas and London when compared with those who could afford such an expense. This association was not seen in rural areas, suggesting that being able to afford an unexpected payment has a lower impact on happiness there.

Adults who do not expect to be able to save any money over the next 12 months were significantly linked to lower levels of happiness than those who could, in all areas. This trend was strongest in urban areas and the percentage of people who expect not to be able to save was even across each area (31%).

More information about the impact of the coronavirus pandemic on household finances and well-being can be found in Personal and economic well-being in Great Britain: May 2021 (https://www.ons.gov.uk/peoplepopulationandcommunity/wellbeing/bulletins/personalande conomicwellbeingintheuk/may2021).

Demographic variables

Figure 4: When compared to adults over the age of 75, all other age groups were linked to lower levels of happiness

Rural and urban areas, 7 January to 28 March 2021

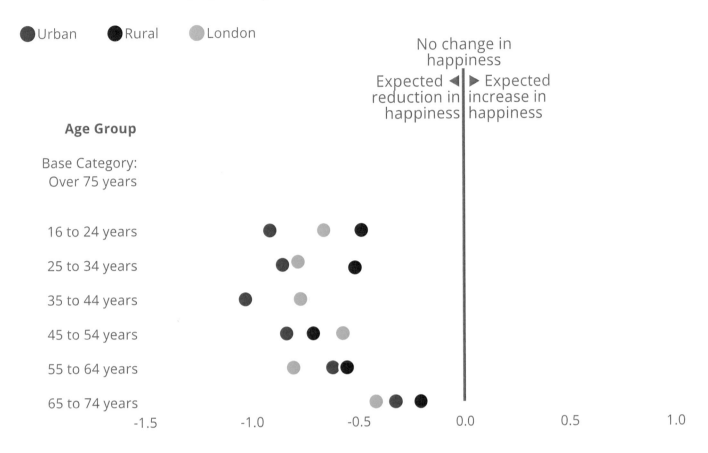

Embed code

Source: Office for National Statistics – Opinions and Lifestyle Survey

Download the data (https://www.ons.gov.uk/visualisations/dvc1304/age/datadownload.xlsx)

Notes

1. The 2011 Rural/Urban classification was used to create the rural and urban classes, more information on this can be found here: 2011 rural/urban classification - Office for National Statistics (https://www.ons.gov.uk/methodology/geography/geographicalproducts/ruralurbanclassifications/2011ruralurbanclassification).

2. The results shown in Figure 4 are statistically significant at the 5% level unless mentioned.

Age group

When compared with the reference group of respondents aged 75 years or over, all younger adults across all areas had significantly lower levels of happiness, with the effect being greater in urban areas than rural areas. This indicates that people over the age of 75 years are most likely to report the highest level of happiness, especially compared with those aged 35 to 44 years. This trend is visible in previous publications on well-being (https://www.ons.gov.uk/peoplepopulationandcommunity/wellbeing/articles/personalandec onomicwellbeingintheuk/whatmattersmosttoourlifesatisfaction), which reported higher well-being in both young adults and older respondents, and lower well-being at peak working age. This may be partly explained by demographic differences where London had the fewest adults aged 75 years or over (7%), compared with 10% in urban areas, and 14% in rural areas.

5. Happiness in local authorities

Figure 5: Personal happiness scores and factors linked to lower happiness by local authority, January to March 2021

Local authorities, 7 January to 28 March 2021

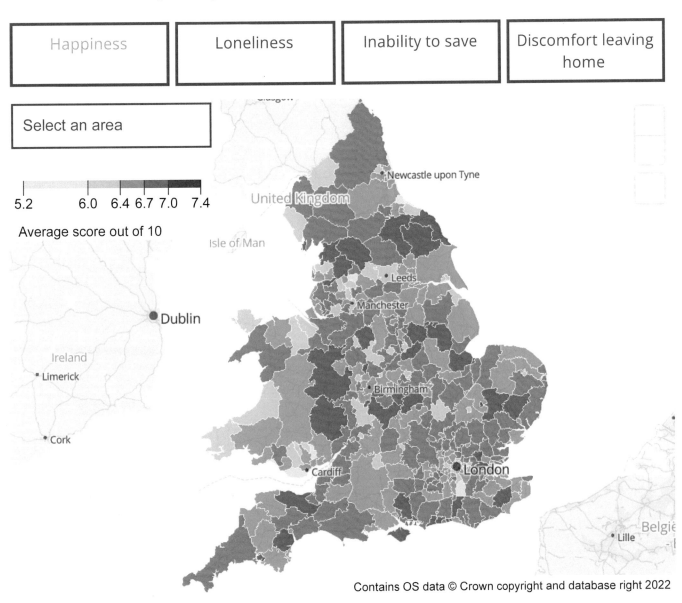

Contains OS data © Crown copyright and database right 2022

Source: Office for National Statistics - Opinions and lifestyle survey

Embed code

Note: This is a snapshot of an interactive image, to view the full image please go to: https://www.ons.gov.uk/peoplepopulationandcommunity/wellbeing/bulletins/coronavirusandcontributorstosubnationalwellbeing/januarytomarch2021

Download the data

(https://www.ons.gov.uk/visualisations/dvc1304/map/datadownload.xlsx)

Notes

1. Question: "Overall, how happy did you feel yesterday, where 0 is 'not at all happy' and 10 is 'completely happy'?"

2. Question: "And how often do you feel lonely?"

3. Question: "At this time, how comfortable or uncomfortable do you feel about leaving your home due to the coronavirus (COVID-19) pandemic?"

4. Question: "In view of the general economic situation, do you think you will be able to save any money in the next twelve months?"

5. Confidence intervals are provided in the datasets associated with this bulletin. As a general rule, if the confidence interval around one estimate overlaps with the interval around another, we cannot say with certainty that there is more than a chance difference between the two estimates.

6. Because of small sample sizes and large confidence intervals, local authorities should not be ranked against each other.

6. Coronavirus and subnational well-being data

Coronavirus and contributors to subnational well-being by local authority
(https://www.ons.gov.uk/peoplepopulationandcommunity/wellbeing/datasets/coronavir
usandcontributorstosubnationalwellbeingbylocalauthorityjanuarytomarch2021)
Dataset | Released 26 May 2021
Indicators from the Opinions and Lifestyle Survey (OPN) on factors related to well-being
by local authority.

Coronavirus and contributors to subnational well-being, mean happiness
(https://www.ons.gov.uk/peoplepopulationandcommunity/wellbeing/datasets/coronavir
usandcontributorstosubnationalwellbeingmeanhappinessjanuarytomarch2021)
Dataset | Released 26 May 2021
Mean happiness indicators from the Opinions and Lifestyle Survey (OPN) on factors
related to well-being in rural areas, urban areas and London.

Coronavirus and contributors to subnational well-being, percentage estimates
(https://www.ons.gov.uk/peoplepopulationandcommunity/wellbeing/datasets/coronavir
usandcontributorstosubnationalwellbeingpercentageestimatesjanuarytomarch2021)
Dataset | Released 26 May 2021
Indicators from the Opinions and Lifestyle Survey (OPN) on factors related to well-being
in rural areas, urban areas and London.

7. Glossary

Happiness

Our personal happiness measure asks people to evaluate how happy they felt yesterday on a scale of 0 to 10. Happiness is one of four Office for National Statistics (ONS) well-being measures, with more information available in personal well-being user guidance (https://www.ons.gov.uk/peoplepopulationandcommunity/wellbeing/methodologies/personalwellbeingsurveyuserguide).

Early 2021 lockdown

On 5 January 2021, the UK government announced a national lockdown for England. Similar rules applied for Scotland and Wales, particularly the message to "stay at home" meaning that adults in Great Britain were under a national lockdown at the start of the year in 2021.

On 22 February 2021, the UK government published a four-step roadmap for easing lockdown restrictions in England. On 23 February, the Scottish government published an update to the strategic framework for easing lockdown restrictions in Scotland.

In England, per the first step of easing outlined in the roadmap, people could meet outdoors in a group of six from 29 March (among other changes to restrictions). In Wales, from 13 March, "stay at home" restrictions were replaced with "stay local" restrictions. In Scotland, "stay local" replaced "stay at home" from 2 April.

Further easing of lockdown restrictions were applied from 12 April in England, Wales and Scotland. The data presented in this release were collected prior to this.

Rural versus urban

The 2011 rural-urban classification (https://www.ons.gov.uk/methodology/geography/geographicalproducts/ruralurbanclassifications/2011ruralurbanclassification) is used to classify areas based upon whether they are predominantly urban, or rural, in composition. In this analysis, we made use of the RUC2011, a suite of classifications produced based upon the 2011 Census at the output area geographic level.

Code	Detail	Broad category
A1	Urban major conurbation	Urban
B1	Urban minor conurbation	Urban
C1	Urban city and town	Urban
C2	Urban city and town in a sparse setting	Urban
D1	Rural town and fringe	Rural
D2	Rural town and fringe in a sparse setting	Rural
E1	Rural village	Rural
E2	Rural village in a sparse setting	Rural
F1	Rural hamlet and isolated dwellings	Rural
F2	Rural hamlet and isolated dwellings in a sparse setting	Rural

Given that virtually the whole of London is classified as an urban area, and that London produces different results in comparison to other urban areas, we separated London as a distinct geography. The results for rural areas for the entire country would include a very small amount of London's value, and the results for urban areas for the entire country would include almost the entirety of London's value.

8. Measuring the data

The Opinions and Lifestyle Survey (OPN) is a monthly omnibus survey. In response to the coronavirus (COVID-19) pandemic, we have adapted the OPN to become a weekly survey used to collect data on the impact of the coronavirus on day-to-day life in Great Britain.

A sample of households was randomly selected from those that had previously completed the Labour Force Survey (LFS) or the Labour Market Survey (LMS), and from each household one adult was selected to complete the survey. This table provides information on collection dates, sample sizes and response rates of the data used for the analysis in this bulletin.

Pooled Dataset	Collection start	Collection End	Responses Received	Sample Size	Response Rate
Spring 2020 lockdown	20/03/2020	31/05/2020	14,049	23,299	60.3
Summer 2020	04/06/2020	02/08/2020	15,660	23,838	65.7
Autumn 2020 restrictions	05/08/2020	11/10/2020	12,807	19,611	65.3
Winter 2020 lockdowns	14/10/2020	03/01/2021	41,245	63,158	65.3
Early 2021 lockdown	07/01/2021	28/03/2021	52,331	72,439	72.2

To enable more detailed analysis, such as the breakdowns included in this bulletin, waves of the weekly OPN data have been pooled together to create larger datasets. By pooling data, we improve the sample size available to create smaller breakdowns of individual questions at the expense of having to report on a wider time period. Survey weights were applied to responses in each pooled dataset such that the weighted estimates are representative of the adult population of Great Britain.

Further information on the survey design and quality can be found in the <u>Opinions and Lifestyle Survey Quality and Methodology Information.</u> <u>(https://www.ons.gov.uk/peoplepopulationandcommunity/healthandsocialcare/healthandlif eexpectancies/methodologies/opinionsandlifestylesurveyqmi)</u>

Where differences between groups or geographies are presented in this bulletin, the significance of this difference is indicated, and associated <u>confidence intervals</u> <u>(https://www.ons.gov.uk/methodology/methodologytopicsandstatisticalconcepts/uncertaint yandhowwemeasureit#confidence-interval)</u> are included in the datasets associated with this bulletin.

Methodology

We used regression analysis as it can measure the size and strength of a relationship between two variables, while holding all other factors in the model constant. This is important when analysing the difference between rural areas, urban areas and London as there are differences in the populations in each area which may be causing the differences in average well-being.

While regression analysis provides information on the strength, size and direction of a relationship between two variables, it cannot prove that there is causation. Our regression models explained between 16% and 22% of the differences in happiness. This is to be expected as research has suggested that <u>genetic and personality factors account for around half of the differences in personal well-being. (https://www.nature.com/articles/s41598-018-29881-x)</u> The model has been presented to highlight associations between predictor variables and well-being, but is not suitable for predictive purposes.

The predictor variables here are categorical, so the regression outputs show the expected difference in well-being for a person being in the reference category compared with each other category with other factors held constant. The reference categories for each variable in these models were chosen to highlight the more relevant direction of association.

Separate regressions were run on subsets of the dataset to understand the expected differences in happiness for each variable in rural areas, urban areas and London so we can investigate which factors may be affecting happiness in these areas.

Ordinary Least Squares versus Logistic regression

Ordinary Least Squares (OLS) was the chosen regression model over logistic regression for ease of interpretation and because it preserves the detail of the results. Logistic regression would require the well-being responses to be grouped, into "high" and "low" categories, for instance, this would remove some of the detail from the result as any regression would only estimate somebody moving from the high to low category or vice versa.

An important assumption in OLS regression is that the dependent variable is continuous. The personal well-being survey responses, however, are discrete on a 1 to 10 scale. OLS regression also assumes that the values of the dependent variable (for example, personal well-being ratings) are cardinal (that is, the interval between any pair of categories such as between 2 and 3 is of the same magnitude as the interval between any other similar pair such as between 6 and 7), which we cannot be certain of.

However, OLS may still be implemented when there are more than five levels of the ordered categorical responses, particularly when there is a clear ordering of the categories as is the case for the happiness variable.

Controlling for variables

This bulletin has focused on the factors that were most relevant to the Coronavirus (COVID-19) pandemic. The following list of variables were also controlled for in the model to ensure accuracy:

- sex

- household type

- ethnicity

- education status

- tenure

- marital status

- disability status

- city region (urban regression)

- NUTS2 region (London regression)

- NUTS1 region (rural regression)

- health condition

9. Strengths and limitations

The main strengths of the Opinions and Lifestyle Survey (OPN) include:

- it allows for timely production of data and statistics that can respond quickly to changing needs.

- it meets data needs: the questionnaire is developed with customer consultation, and design expertise is applied in the development stages.

- robust methods are adopted for the survey's sampling and weighting strategies to limit the impact of bias.

- quality assurance procedures are undertaken throughout the analysis stages to minimise the risk of error.

The main limitations of the OPN include:

- analysis of estimates in Wales and Scotland are based on low sample sizes, and therefore caution should be used with these estimates.

- comparisons between periods and groups must be done with caution as estimates are provided from a sample survey; as such, confidence intervals are included in the datasets to present the sampling variability, which should be taken into account when assessing differences between periods, as true differences may not exist.

10. Related links

Well-being latest data and analysis
(https://www.ons.gov.uk/peoplepopulationandcommunity/wellbeing/articles/coronaviru
sandanxietygreatbritain/3april2020to10may2020)
Web page | Updated as data become available
Latest data and analysis on societal and personal well-being in the UK looking beyond
what we produce, to areas such as health, relationships, education and skills, what we
do, where we live, our finances and the environment.

Coronavirus (COVID-19) latest data and analysis (http://www.ons.gov.uk/coronavirus)
Web page | Updated as data become available
Latest data and analysis on the coronavirus (COVID-19) pandemic in the UK and its
effects on the economy and society.

Coronavirus and social impacts on households in subnational areas in Great Britain:
2020 and 2021
(https://www.ons.gov.uk/peoplepopulationandcommunity/healthandsocialcare/healtha
ndwellbeing/bulletins/coronavirusandthesocialimpactsonhouseholdsinsubnationalarea
singreatbritain/2020and2021)
Bulletin | Released 27 April 2021
Indicators from the Office for National Statistics (ONS) Opinions and Lifestyle Survey to
understand the impacts of the coronavirus (COVID-19) pandemic on different
households in subnational areas in Great Britain.

Coronavirus and the social impacts on NUTS2 areas in Great Britain
(https://www.ons.gov.uk/peoplepopulationandcommunity/healthandsocialcare/healtha
ndwellbeing/datasets/coronavirusandthesocialimpactsonnuts2areasingreatbritain)
Dataset| Released 27 November 2020
Indicators from the Opinions and Lifestyle Survey (OPN) on the impact of the
coronavirus (COVID-19) on people, households and communities, by NUTS2 area.

Coronavirus and the social impacts on the countries and regions of Britain: April 2020
(https://www.ons.gov.uk/peoplepopulationandcommunity/healthandsocialcare/healtha
ndwellbeing/bulletins/coronavirusandthesocialimpactsonthecountriesandregionsofbrita
in/april2020)

Bulletin | Released 26 May 2020

Indicators from the OPN to understand the impact of the coronavirus pandemic on people, households and communities in the countries and regions of Great Britain. This release uses four waves of survey results covering April 2020 to present results for Wales, Scotland and the nine English regions.

Contact details for this statistical bulletin

Will Haste
cities@ons.gov.uk
Telephone: +44 (0)20 8039 0369

Office for National Statistics

Data and analysis from Census 2021

Unity and division in Great Britain: 24 April to 28 June 2020

The effect of the coronavirus (COVID-19) pandemic on perceptions of unity and division in Great Britain, using the weekly Opinions and Lifestyle Survey (OPN). Includes an assessment of unity and division over time and across numerous socioeconomic divides, such as age, sex and perceptions of community.

Contact:
Laurence Day and Mark Hamilton

Release date:
25 August 2020

Next release:
To be announced

Table of contents

1. Main points

- Over the period as a whole, from 24 April to 28 June 2020, more adults on average thought that Britain will be united after we have recovered from the coronavirus (COVID-19) pandemic (46%) than thought that we were united before the pandemic (24%).

- In this same period, adults in Scotland were less likely (31%) to say that Britain will be united after the pandemic than those in either England (47%) or Wales (44%).

- Although women were as likely as men to say that Britain was united before the pandemic, they were more likely than men to think that Britain will be united after it, with half (50%) saying that Britain would be either very or somewhat united compared with 41% of men.

- Perceptions of unity within Britain are associated with higher average life satisfaction, happiness and feelings that things done in life are worthwhile as well as with checking on neighbours, feeling like the community is available to support you and thinking people are doing more to help others.

- As time progressed through the period, the percentage of adults who thought that Britain would be more united after the pandemic declined by 29 percentage points (from 57% in the first week of the period to 28% in the last week) so that by the end of this period, there was no difference in the percentage of people who thought that Britain would be united before the pandemic compared with those who thought it would be united after.

- Similarly, as time progressed through the period, there was only a small difference in the proportion of the population who thought that Britain would be equal after the pandemic (22%) compared with those who thought it was equal before (19%).

- Although perceptions of how kind people in Britain will be after we recover from the coronavirus pandemic declined from 67% at the start of the period to 56% at the end of the period, by the end there were still more people who thought that people in Britain would be kind after the pandemic than thought that people were kind before it (46%).

Statistician's comment

"Today's research shows that earlier in the national lockdown, people believed that a post-pandemic Britain would be a more united one.

"However, over subsequent weeks, this belief declined. Most people also expected that inequalities in society would remain. But interestingly, there is still a belief that we will be a kind nation, perhaps because of the many stories of individual kindness we have heard or experienced over this time"

Dawn Snape, Assistant Director, Sustainability and Inequalities Division, Office for National Statistics

2. Understanding the impact on society

This bulletin contains data and indicators from a new module being undertaken through the Office for National Statistics (ONS) Opinions and Lifestyle Survey (OPN) to understand the impact of the coronavirus (COVID-19) pandemic on British society.

The statistics in this publication are based on pooled data from the OPN weekly survey of adults aged 16 years and over in Great Britain, which includes England, Scotland and Wales.

The period covered by this bulletin is between 24 April and 28 June 2020 (inclusive). This includes two weeks during the national lockdown and seven weeks during which lockdown restrictions were eased at different rates across the countries of Great Britain.

The bulletin focuses on responses to six questions:

- How united or divided do you think Britain was before the coronavirus (COVID-19) outbreak?

- How united or divided do you think Britain will be after we have recovered from the coronavirus (COVID-19) outbreak?

- How equal or unequal do you think Britain was before the coronavirus (COVID-19) outbreak?

- How equal or unequal do you think Britain will be after we have recovered from coronavirus (COVID-19) outbreak?

- How kind or unkind do you think people in Britain were before the coronavirus (COVID-19) outbreak?

- How kind or unkind do you think people in Britain will be after we have recovered from the coronavirus (COVID-19) outbreak?

For ease of interpretation, responses to each question have been combined into four responses: "very or somewhat united/equal/kind"; "very or somewhat divided/unequal/unkind"; "neither united nor divided/equal nor unequal/kind nor unkind"; and "don't know/prefer not to say".

It should be noted that the initial question in each case is retrospective, asking respondents to think about a time before the coronavirus pandemic. The second question asks about expectations of the future. The survey asked different people their views each week over the period covered, so the findings reflect the views of a representative sample of people in Great Britain each week during that period. They do not reflect changing views of the same individuals over time.

Results are based on 12,630 responding adults over the whole period. We also include statistics based on the individual weekly surveys over this period to show how responses have changed over time. Throughout this bulletin, "this period" refers to the period from 24 April to 28 June 2020. Where data for particular weeks are used, the dates are noted separately.

This bulletin presents a summary of results, with further data including confidence intervals (https://www.ons.gov.uk/methodology/methodologytopicsandstatisticalconcepts/uncertaint yandhowwemeasureit#confidence-interval) for the estimates contained in the associated dataset (http://dataset). Throughout the bulletin, we only comment on findings that are statistically significant (https://www.ons.gov.uk/methodology/methodologytopicsandstatisticalconcepts/uncertaint yandhowwemeasureit#statistical-significance). The statistics presented are estimates and as with all estimates, there is a level of uncertainty (https://www.ons.gov.uk/methodology/methodologytopicsandstatisticalconcepts/uncertaint yandhowwemeasureit#what-is-uncertainty) associated with them. Where available, 95% confidence intervals have been shown. These indicate the range within which we would expect the true value to lie for 95 out of every 100 samples drawn at random from the population. Wide confidence intervals, often associated with small sample sizes or large sample variance, indicate a wider range of values within which we would expect the true value to lie.

Throughout this bulletin, we have assessed statistical significance using non-overlapping confidence intervals. This method has the limitation that some estimates with overlapping confidence intervals may be significantly different but will not be identified as such (that is, the false-negative rate will be inflated).

Only statistically significant differences are commented on in this release. Caution should therefore be exercised when making other comparisons between groups or time periods as observed differences may not be statistically significant.

3. Expectations of a united Britain

Figure 1 shows that across the period from the end of April to the end of June, more people thought that Britain would be united after we have recovered from the coronavirus (COVID-19) pandemic (46%) than thought it was united before the pandemic (24%).

Figure 1: Almost half of respondents thought that Britain would be united after the coronavirus pandemic compared with less than a quarter who thought it was united before

Percentage of people reporting different levels of unity in Britain before and after the coronavirus pandemic, Great Britain, 24 April to 28 June 2020

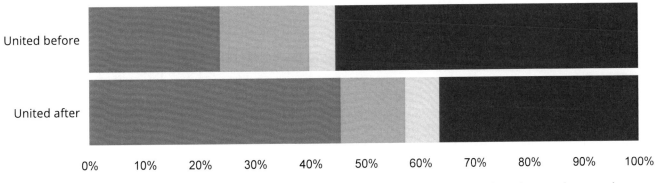

Source: Office for National Statistics – Opinions and Lifestyle Survey

Embed code

Download the data (https://www.ons.gov.uk/visualisations/dvc947/fig1/datadownload.xlsx)

Notes:

1. Responses for very united and somewhat united, very divided and somewhat divided, and don't know and prefer not to say have been combined.

2. The question "How united or divided do you think Britain was before the coronavirus (COVID-19) outbreak?" is asked retrospectively.

3. The data included in this chart use a pooled dataset covering the period 24 April to 28 June 2020.

4. Base population for percentage: adults aged 16 years or over.

5. Percentages may not add up to 100 because of rounding.

Where we live

Considering the impact of the coronavirus pandemic on perceptions of unity across the different countries of Great Britain, although across all three countries significantly more people expected Britain to be united after the pandemic than felt it was united before, these figures are significantly lower for those in Scotland than those in either England or Wales (Figure 2). Almost half of those in England and Wales (47% and 44% respectively) thought that Britain will be united after we have recovered from the coronavirus pandemic, compared with less than a third of people in Scotland (31%).

Figure 2: Although people in Scotland were more likely to think that Britain will be united after the coronavirus pandemic than think it was united before, they were less likely to say this than those in England or Wales

Percentage of people reporting different levels of unity in Britain before and after the coronavirus pandemic by country, Great Britain, 24 April to 28 June 2020

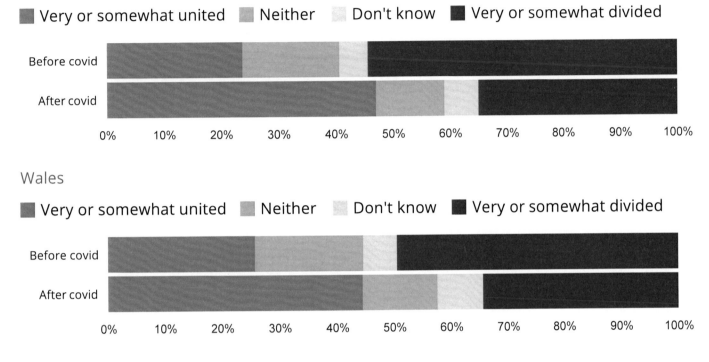

England

■ Very or somewhat united   ■ Neither   □ Don't know   ■ Very or somewhat divided

Wales

■ Very or somewhat united   ■ Neither   □ Don't know   ■ Very or somewhat divided

Scotland

■ Very or somewhat united   ■ Neither   □ Don't know   ■ Very or somewhat divided

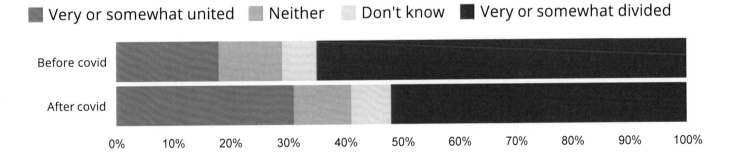

Notes:

1. Responses for very united and somewhat united, very divided and somewhat divided, and don't know and prefer not to say have been combined.

2. The question "How united or divided do you think Britain was before the coronavirus (COVID-19) outbreak?" is asked retrospectively.

3. The data included in this chart use a pooled dataset covering the period 24 April to 28 June 2020.

4. Base population for percentage: adults aged 16 years or over.

5. Percentages may not add up to 100 because of rounding.

Sex

Perceptions of unity in Britain have been more positively impacted by the pandemic among women than men (Figure 3). While similar proportions of men and women, around a quarter, thought that Britain was united before the pandemic, significantly more women than men thought that it will be united after we have recovered from it (50% and 41%, respectively). Women were also significantly less likely than men to think that Britain was divided before the pandemic and fewer thought that Britain will be divided after we have recovered from it.

Figure 3: Men were more likely than women to think that Britain was divided before the pandemic and that Britain will be divided after we recover from it

Perceptions of unity and division before and after the coronavirus pandemic by sex, Great Britain, 24 April to 28 June 2020

Males

■ Very or somewhat united   ■ Neither   □ Don't know   ■ Very or somewhat divided

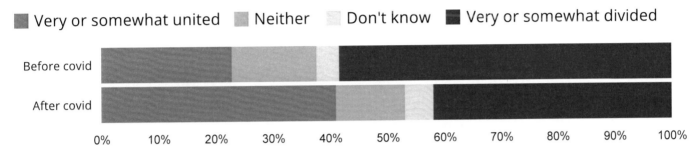

Females

■ Very or somewhat united   ■ Neither   □ Don't know   ■ Very or somewhat divided

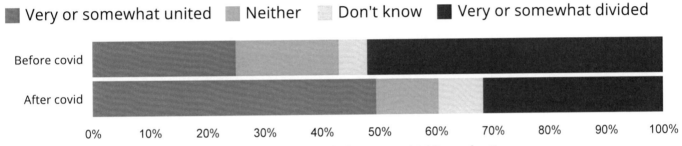

Source: Office for National Statistics – Opinions and Lifestyle Survey

Notes:

1. Responses for very united and somewhat united, very divided and somewhat divided, and don't know and prefer not to say have been combined.

2. The question "How united or divided do you think Britain was before the coronavirus (COVID-19) outbreak?" is asked retrospectively.

3. The data included in this chart use a pooled dataset covering the period 24 April to 28 June 2020.

4. Base population for percentage: adults aged 16 years or over.

5. Percentages may not add up to 100 because of rounding.

Age

Around 3 in 10 adults aged 65 years and over thought that Britain was united before the pandemic compared with around a fifth of those aged between 25 and 64 years. However, although the pandemic has had a positive impact on perceptions of unity across all age groups, with more people of all ages thinking that Britain will be united after we have recovered from the pandemic, only around 41% of 25- to 44-year-olds thought this compared with almost half of those aged 45 years and over (Figure 4).

Figure 4: Perceptions of division after the coronavirus pandemic were greater for those aged 25 to 44 years than any other age groups

Perceptions of unity and division after the coronavirus pandemic by age, Great Britain, 24 April to 28 June 2020

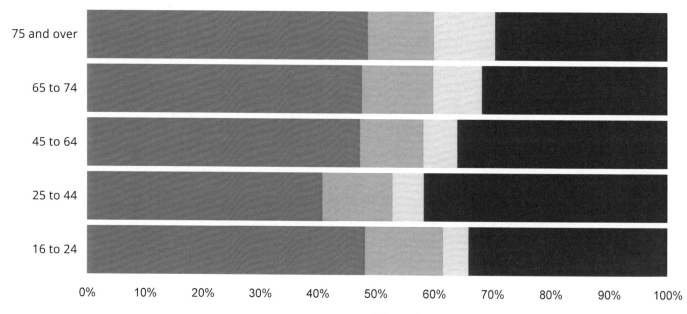

Source: Office for National Statistics – Opinions and Lifestyle Survey

Embed code

Download the data (https://www.ons.gov.uk/visualisations/dvc947/fig4/datadownload.xlsx)

Notes:

1. Responses for very united and somewhat united, very divided and somewhat divided, and don't know and prefer not to say have been combined.

2. The data included in this chart use a pooled dataset covering the period 24 April to 28 June 2020.

3. Base population for percentage: adults aged 16 years or over.

4. Percentages may not add up to 100 because of rounding.

4. Perceptions of unity and personal well-being

Perceptions of unity and division have a clear link to personal well-being. Average ratings of life satisfaction, feeling that things done in life are worthwhile and happiness are consistently higher among those who think that Britain was united before the pandemic compared with those who think it was divided as well as among those who think that Britain will be united after we recover from it compared with those who think it will be divided (Figure 5).

Those who think Britain will be united after the pandemic on average rated their life satisfaction as 7.2 out of 10 compared with 6.8 among those who think Britain will be divided. Similarly, feeling that things done in life are worthwhile was on average rated as 7.6 among with those who thought Britain will be united after the coronavirus (COVID-19) pandemic compared with 7.2 for those who thought that Britain will be divided, and happiness received ratings of 7.2 and 6.8 out of 10 respectively. There was no difference in average ratings of anxiety between the two groups.

Among respondents with very high life satisfaction, 53% thought that Britain will be united after the pandemic compared with only 29% of those with low life satisfaction.

Figure 5: Those who thought Britain will be united after the coronavirus pandemic had higher average ratings of life satisfaction, feelings that things done in life are worthwhile and happiness than those who thought Britain will be divided

Average ratings of life satisfaction, feeling that things done in life are worthwhile, happiness and anxiety by response to unity after the coronavirus pandemic question, Great Britain, 24 April to 28 June 2020

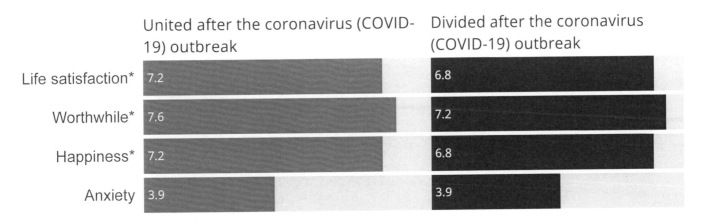

	United after the coronavirus (COVID-19) outbreak	Divided after the coronavirus (COVID-19) outbreak
Life satisfaction*	7.2	6.8
Worthwhile*	7.6	7.2
Happiness*	7.2	6.8
Anxiety	3.9	3.9

Source: Office for National Statistics – Opinions and Lifestyle Survey

Notes:

1. Each well-being question is asked on a scale from 0 to 10, where 0 is "not at all" and 10 is "completely".

2. Responses for very united and somewhat united, very divided and somewhat divided, and don't know and prefer not to say have been combined.

3. The data included in this chart use a pooled dataset covering the period 24 April to 28 June 2020.

4. Base population for percentage: adults aged 16 years or over.

5. "*" shows where significant differences have been found between the well-being of those who felt that Britain would be united compared with those who felt that Britain would be divided after the coronavirus pandemic.

The relationship between well-being and perceived unity noted here is similar to findings in our technical report on optimism and personal well-being (https://www.ons.gov.uk/peoplepopulationandcommunity/wellbeing/methodologies/optimis mandpersonalwellbeingtechnicalreport). Specifically, those who were optimistic about the future of the UK reported higher life satisfaction on average than those who were pessimistic. Further supporting this relationship, those who were optimistic about how quickly we would return to normal, reporting less than six months following the coronavirus pandemic, were more likely to report that we will be united (49%) than those who were more pessimistic (41%), reporting over a year or never.

Respondents who reported feeling hardly ever or never lonely were more likely (63%) to have felt that Britain was united before the pandemic, compared with those who reported feeling lonely often or always (54%). However, perceptions of unity after the pandemic did not significantly differ among those people who reported differing degrees of loneliness. Of those who reported feeling lonely often and always, perceptions of unity differed by 26 percentage points between the two questions, before and after the pandemic (compared with 21 percentage points for those who hardly ever or never felt lonely).

5. Perceptions of unity and division linked to respondent's views on society

In this section, we explore how views and actions within our communities are related to a perceived sense of unity in Britain. We also look at how a sense of being well-informed about the pandemic is associated with views about unity or division.

Community support and engagement

Perceptions of community cohesion and support are significantly associated with expectations of unity in Britain after the coronavirus (COVID-19) pandemic. For example, around half (51%) of respondents who agreed that "if they needed help, other local community members would support them" thought that Britain will be united after the coronavirus pandemic, compared with only 26% who disagreed.

Furthermore, 51% of those who reported having checked on a neighbour at least once in the past seven days thought that Britain will be united after the pandemic, compared with 40% of those who reported not having checked on neighbours in the past week. Similarly, those who thought that people were doing things to help others more since the coronavirus pandemic were much more likely to expect Britain to be united (51%) after the pandemic has passed than those who thought people were doing less to help others (19%) or the same (24%).

Figure 6: People with perceptions of neighbourliness and people helping others out more were more likely to think that Britain will be united after the coronavirus pandemic than on average in Great Britain

Percentage of respondents who think that Great Britain will be united after the coronavirus pandemic, Great Britain, 24 April to 28 June 2020

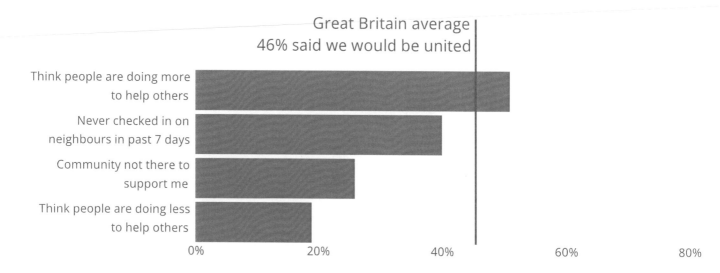

Source: Office for National Statistics – Opinions and Lifestyle Survey

Notes:

1. The percentages shown in this chart are the proportion of respondents that felt that Great Britain would be "Very/somewhat" united after the coronavirus pandemic.

2. Responses for very united and somewhat united have been combined.

3. The data included in this chart use a pooled dataset covering the period 24 April to 28 June 2020.

4. Base population for percentage: adults aged 16 years or over.

Sufficient information to stay safe

A sense of being fully informed and understanding how to avoid catching COVID-19 is also associated with expectations of a united Britain, while a perceived lack of information is associated with expectations of a divided country.

Respondents who reported that they had enough information to protect themselves from COVID-19 were more likely (47%) to say that Britain will be united after the coronavirus pandemic than those who said they did not have enough information (33%).

Figure 7: Those who felt they had enough information to protect themselves from COVID-19 were more likely to report that they thought Britain will be united after the coronavirus pandemic than those who did not

Perceptions of unity and division after the coronavirus pandemic by perceptions on having sufficient information to stay safe, Great Britain, 24 April to 28 June 2020

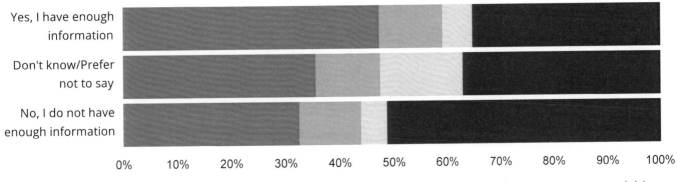

Source: Office for National Statistics – Opinions and Lifestyle Survey

Embed code

Download the data (https://www.ons.gov.uk/visualisations/dvc947/fig7/datadownload.xlsx)

Notes:

1. Responses for very united and somewhat united, very divided and somewhat divided, and don't know and prefer not to say have been combined.

2. The data included in this chart use a pooled dataset covering the period 24 April to 28 June 2020.

3. Base population for percentage: adults aged 16 years or over.

4. Percentages may not add up to 100 because of rounding.

6. Shifting perceptions of unity and division in Britain

While findings on perceptions of unity and division among all of those surveyed between late April and late June suggest that the pandemic may have contributed to a greater sense of us all being in it together, looking at the changes week on week reveals that expectations that Britain will be united after the coronavirus (COVID-19) pandemic declined significantly over this period, while expectations that it will be divided increased (Figure 8).

While perceptions of unity in Britain before the pandemic have remained fairly stable over time, expectations of a united Britain after the pandemic declined by 29 percentage points between 24 April and 28 June 2020, and expectations of a divided Britain increased by 33 percentage points over the same period. This suggests a shift in expectations about the future of British society as we moved through the lockdown and into the progressive easing of restrictions.

In fact, in the latest period for which data are available (25 to 28 June), there is no significant difference in the proportion of people who think that Britain was united before the pandemic as think that it will be united after we recover from it. The same is true when comparing the proportions of the population who think that Britain was divided before the pandemic as think it will be divided when we emerge from it. This suggests that any increases in perceptions of unity that were experienced during lockdown have gradually dissipated as things have slowly started to return to normal.

Figure 8: Perceptions of unity after the coronavirus pandemic have declined over time, while those of division have increased over the same period

Percentage of people reporting different levels of unity in Britain after the coronavirus pandemic across time, Great Britain, 24 April to 28 June 2020

■ Very or somewhat united   ■ Neither   ■ Don't know   ■ Very or somewhat divided

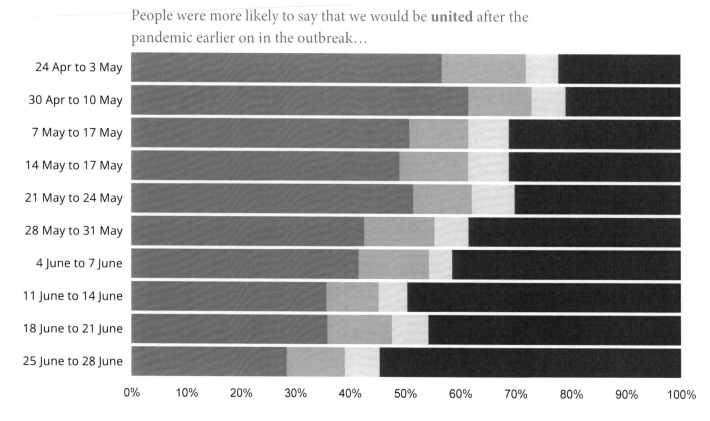

Source: Office for National Statistics – Opinions and Lifestyle Survey

Notes:

1. Responses for very united and somewhat united, very divided and somewhat divided, and don't know and prefer not to say have been combined.

2. The data used in this chart come from 10 individual waves of data collected from 24 April to 3 May and 25 June to 28 June.

3. Base population for percentage: adults aged 16 years or over.

4. Percentages may not add up to 100 because of rounding.

7. Perceptions of equality and kindness in Britain

While perceptions of a united Great Britain after the coronavirus (COVID-19) pandemic declined between 24 April and 28 June 2020, perceptions of how equal Britain will be after the coronavirus pandemic remained broadly stable week on week and over the period as a whole; there was only a small difference in the proportion of the population who thought that Britain was equal before the pandemic (19%) and the proportion who thought that it will be equal after we recover from the pandemic (22%) (Figure 9). Together, these findings suggest that the pandemic has not impacted on perceptions of inequalities in society to the same extent as it did on perceptions of unity.

Figure 9: Slightly more people thought that Britain will be equal after the pandemic than thought it was equal before

Percentage of people reporting different levels of equality in Britain before and after the coronavirus pandemic, Great Britain, 24 April to 28 June 2020

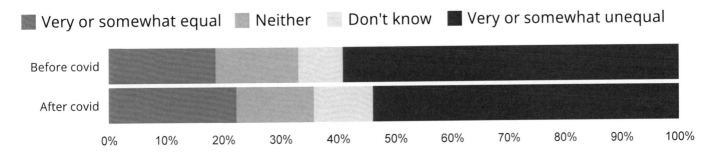

Embed code

Download the data (https://www.ons.gov.uk/visualisations/dvc947/fig9/datadownload.xlsx)

Notes:

1. Responses for very equal and somewhat equal, very unequal and somewhat unequal, and don't know and prefer not to say have been combined.

2. The data included in this chart use a pooled dataset covering the period 24 April to 28 June 2020.

3. Questions asked are: "How equal or unequal do you think Britain was before the coronavirus (COVID-19) outbreak?" and "How equal or unequal do you think Britain will be after we have recovered from the coronavirus (COVID-19) outbreak?".

4. Base population for percentage: adults aged 16 years or over.

5. Percentages may not add up to 100 because of rounding.

Looking at perceptions of kindness in British society, for the period as a whole, significantly more people think that people will be kind in Britain after we have recovered from the coronavirus pandemic (63%) compared with those who think that people in Britain were kind before the pandemic (44%) (Figure 10). However, perceptions of kindness declined over this time, from 67% at the start of the period to 56% by the end. Although this is similar to the pattern seen for perceptions of unity, at the end of the period there were still significantly more people who thought that people in Britain will be kind after we emerge from the pandemic than thought that people in Britain were kind before it.

Figure 10: More people thought that people in Great Britain will be kind after the coronavirus pandemic than thought people were kind before it.

Percentage of people reporting different levels of kindness in Britain before and after the coronavirus pandemic, Great Britain, 24 April to 28 June 2020

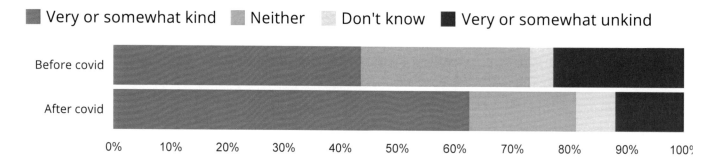

Source: Office for National Statistics – Opinions and Lifestyle Survey

Embed code

Download the data (https://www.ons.gov.uk/visualisations/dvc947/fig10/datadownload.xlsx)

Notes:

1. Responses for very kind and somewhat kind, very unkind and somewhat unkind, and don't know and prefer not to say have been combined.

2. The data included in this chart use a pooled dataset covering the period 24 April to 28 June 2020.

3. Questions asked are: "How kind or unkind do you think people in Britain were before the coronavirus (COVID-19) outbreak?" and "How kind or unkind do you think Britain will be after we have recovered from the coronavirus (COVID-19) outbreak?".

4. Base population for percentage: adults aged 16 years or over.

5. Percentages may not add up to 100 because of rounding.

As might be expected, perceptions of equality and kindness are associated with perceptions of unity. Significantly more of those who thought that Britain will be equal after the coronavirus pandemic (80%) also thought that Britain will be united, compared with those who thought that Britain will be divided (13%). Similarly, 59% of those who thought that people in Britain will be kind after the coronavirus pandemic thought that Britain will be united, compared with 28% who thought it will be divided.

8. Unity and division data

Estimates of unity, equality and kindness
(https://www.ons.gov.uk/peoplepopulationandcommunity/wellbeing/datasets/estimates
ofunityequalityandkindness)
Dataset | Released 25 August 2020
Estimates of unity, equality and kindness in Britain before and after the coronavirus (COVID-19) pandemic, with breakdowns of unity by social groups, countries and regions of Great Britain, personal well-being, and perceptions of society.

9. Glossary

Personal well-being

Our personal well-being measures ask people to evaluate, on a scale of 0 to 10, how satisfied they are with their life overall, whether they feel they have meaning and purpose in their life, and their emotions (happiness and anxiety) during a particular period.

Lockdown

Lockdown is the shutting down of all non-essential activities to slow the spread of the coronavirus (COVID-19). In the UK, this had seen strict limits imposed on daily life, including:

- people ordered to only leave the house for essentials such as food, medicine, exercise or to care for a vulnerable person

- the closure of non-essential shops

- the banning of gatherings of more than two people

The UK lockdown was applied on 23 March 2020. This has formed the basis for each nation's Stay at home guidance. Specific Stay at home guidance for England (https://www.gov.uk/government/publications/covid-19-stay-at-home-guidance/stay-at-home-guidance-for-households-with-possible-coronavirus-covid-19-infection), Scotland (https://www.gov.scot/publications/coronavirus-covid-19-staying-at-home-and-away-from-others-social-distancing/pages/staying-at-home/), Wales (https://gov.wales/staying-home-and-away-others-guidance) and Northern Ireland (https://www.nidirect.gov.uk/articles/coronavirus-covid-19-staying-home-and-self-isolation) is available. During the majority of the period covered in this release, all countries of the UK remained in strict lockdown, but from 1 June 2020 the limits in England were relaxed, with groups of up to six people allowed to meet while socially distancing. The data in this release only cover England, Scotland and Wales.

Disability

To define disability in this publication, we refer to the Government Statistical Service (GSS) harmonised "core" definition: (https://gss.civilservice.gov.uk/policy-store/measuring-disability-for-the-equality-act-2010/) this identifies as "disabled" a person who has a physical or mental health condition or illness that has lasted or is expected to last 12 months or more that reduces their ability to carry-out day-to-day activities.

The GSS definition is designed to reflect the definitions that appear in legal terms in the Disability Discrimination Act 1995 (http://www.legislation.gov.uk/ukpga/1995/50/contents) and the subsequent Equality Act 2010 (http://www.legislation.gov.uk/ukpga/2010/15/section/6).

The GSS harmonised questions are asked of the respondent in the survey, meaning that disability status is self-reported.

10. Measuring the data

The Opinions and Lifestyle Survey (OPN) is a monthly omnibus survey. In response to the coronavirus (COVID-19) pandemic, we have adapted the OPN to become a weekly survey used to collect data on the impact of the coronavirus on day-to-day life in Great Britain. Data from the OPN covering the period from 24 April to 28 June 2020 was used in this publication.

The survey results are weighted to be a nationally representative sample for Great Britain, and data are collected using an online self-completion questionnaire. Individuals who did not want to or were unable to complete the survey online had the opportunity to take part over the phone.

Where differences between groups and periods are presented in this bulletin, associated confidence intervals (https://www.ons.gov.uk/methodology/methodologytopicsandstatisticalconcepts/uncertaintyandhowwemeasureit#confidence-interval), which are included in the associated dataset (http://dataset), indicate their significance.

More quality and methodology information on strengths, limitations, appropriate uses, and how the data were created is available in the OPN QMI (https://www.ons.gov.uk/peoplepopulationandcommunity/healthandsocialcare/healthandlifeexpectancies/methodologies/opinionsandlifestylesurveyqmi).

Sampling

For each wave of the OPN, a sample of 2,500 households was randomly selected from those that had previously completed the Labour Market Survey (LMS). From each household, one adult was selected at random but with unequal probability. Younger people were given higher selection probability than older people because of under-representation in the sample available for the survey.

Further information on the sample design can be found in the OPN QMI (https://www.ons.gov.uk/peoplepopulationandcommunity/healthandsocialcare/healthandlifeexpectancies/methodologies/opinionsandlifestylesurveyqmi).

Weighting

Survey weights were applied to make estimates representative of the population. Weights were first adjusted for non-response and attrition. Subsequently, the weights were calibrated to satisfy population distributions considering the following factors: sex by age, region, tenure, and highest qualification, employment status, National Statistics Socio-economic Classification (NS-SEC) group and smoking status. For age, sex and region, population totals based on projections of mid-year population estimates for May 2020 were used. The resulting weighted sample is therefore representative of the Great Britain adult population by a number of socio-demographic factors and geography.

Next steps

Going forward, we aim to carry out more in-depth analyses to understand more about groups who had differing perceptions of society during lockdown and the period of subsequent easing of lockdown restrictions and how they may have contributed to the different expectations of unity and division in Britain after the coronavirus pandemic.

11. Strengths and limitations

The main strengths of the Opinions and Lifestyle Survey (OPN) include:

- it allows for timely production of data and statistics that can respond quickly to changing needs

- it meets data needs: the questionnaire is developed with customer consultation, and design expertise is applied in the development stages

- robust methods are adopted for the survey's sampling and weighting strategies to limit the impact of bias

- quality assurance procedures are undertaken throughout the analysis stages to minimise the risk of error

The main limitations of the OPN include:

- the sample size is relatively small: 2,500 individuals per week with fewer completed interviews, meaning that detailed analyses for subnational geographies and other sub-groups are not possible unless waves are pooled together and response categories are combined

- comparisons between periods and groups must be done with caution as estimates are provided from a sample survey; as such, confidence intervals (https://www.ons.gov.uk/methodology/methodologytopicsandstatisticalconcepts/uncertaintyandhowwemeasureit#confidence-interval) are included in the datasets to present the sampling variability (https://www.ons.gov.uk/methodology/methodologytopicsandstatisticalconcepts/uncertaintyandhowwemeasureit#sampling-the-population), which should be taken into account when assessing differences between periods, as true differences may not exist

12. Related links

Coronavirus and anxiety, Great Britain: 3 April 2020 to 10 May 2020
(https://www.ons.gov.uk/peoplepopulationandcommunity/wellbeing/articles/coronaviru
sandanxietygreatbritain/3april2020to10may2020)
Article | Released 15 June 2020
The number of people reporting high levels of anxiety has sharply elevated during the
coronavirus (COVID-19) pandemic. This article will provide insights into which socio-
demographic and economic factors were most associated with high levels of anxiety
during the first weeks of lockdown.

Optimism and personal well-being: technical report
(https://www.ons.gov.uk/peoplepopulationandcommunity/wellbeing/methodologies/op
timismandpersonalwellbeingtechnicalreport)
Article | Released 12 March 2020
Exploratory analysis of the relationship between optimism and personal well-being
using questions from the 2019 Opinions and Lifestyle Survey (OPN).

Coronavirus and the social impacts on Great Britain: 7 August 2020
(https://www.ons.gov.uk/peoplepopulationandcommunity/healthandsocialcare/healtha
ndwellbeing/bulletins/coronavirusandthesocialimpactsongreatbritain/7august2020)
Bulletin | Released 7 August 2020
Indicators from the OPN covering the period 29 July to 2 August 2020 to understand the
impact of the coronavirus pandemic on people, households and communities in Great
Britain.

Personal and economic well-being in Great Britain: June 2020
(https://www.ons.gov.uk/peoplepopulationandcommunity/wellbeing/bulletins/personal
andeconomicwellbeingintheuk/june2020)

Bulletin | Released 18 June 2020

Estimates looking across personal and economic well-being covering the period from 20 March to 7 June 2020, to understand the impact of the coronavirus pandemic on people and households in Great Britain.

Contact details for this statistical bulletin

Laurence Day and Mark Hamilton
qualityoflife@ons.gov.uk
Telephone: +44 1633 456300

Coronavirus and clinically extremely vulnerable people in England: 11 October to 16 October 2021

Analysis of clinically extremely vulnerable people in England during the coronavirus (COVID-19) pandemic, including their behaviours and mental and physical well-being.

Contact:

Hannah Mason

Release date:

2 November 2021

Next release:

To be announced

Table of contents

1. Main points

- Most people previously considered to be clinically extremely vulnerable (CEV) to coronavirus (COVID-19) were continuing to take precautions to protect themselves; 22% reported continuing to shield and 68% were no longer shielding but were taking extra precautions.

- The average life satisfaction scores of CEV people were statistically significantly lower for those continuing to shield (6.3 out of 10), compared with those not shielding but taking precautions (7.2) and those not shielding and not taking extra precautions (7.5).

- The majority (94%) of CEV people had left home in the last seven days, a statistically significantly higher proportion compared with previous waves (90%, 21 to 26 June 2021 and 89%, 17 to 22 May 2021, when the shielding guidance had paused but not yet ended).

- A statistically significantly higher proportion of CEV people reported feeling lonely often or always, compared with the general adult population of England (10% and 6% respectively).

Statistician's comment

Tim Gibbs, Head of the Public Service Analysis Team, said:

"Though shielding has ended in England, many clinically extremely vulnerable people have continued to take precautions against COVID-19, with almost one quarter still shielding. This has had an impact on their mental health and well-being, with one in ten reported feeling lonely often or always. I want to thank everyone who has taken part in this survey in helping us to monitor the attitudes and behaviours of the vulnerable."

2. Indicators of clinically extremely vulnerable people's behaviours

In England, 3.7 million people had previously been identified as being clinically extremely vulnerable (CEV) to coronavirus (COVID-19). For more information on identifying CEV people, guidance for clinically extremely vulnerable people, and collecting the data, see the Glossary (https://www.ons.gov.uk/peoplepopulationandcommunity/healthandsocialcare/conditionsa nddiseases/bulletins/coronavirusandclinicallyextremelyvulnerablepeopleinengland/21juneto 26june2021#glossary) and Measuring the data (https://www.ons.gov.uk/peoplepopulationandcommunity/healthandsocialcare/conditionsa nddiseases/bulletins/coronavirusandclinicallyextremelyvulnerablepeopleinengland/21juneto 26june2021#measuring-the-data) sections.

The data reported in this bulletin were collected during a time in which CEV people were not advised to shield and the shielding programme had ended. Care should be taken when comparing wave seven estimates with other waves; data for waves one to three were collected when CEV people were advised to shield. Data for waves four to six were collected when shielding had paused and CEV people were advised to take extra precautions. CEV people are referred to throughout this bulletin; for wave seven this refers to adults previously considered to be CEV.

More about coronavirus

- Find the latest on coronavirus (COVID-19) in the UK (https://www.ons.gov.uk/peoplepopulationandcommunity/healthandsocialcare/con ditionsanddiseases).

- Explore the latest coronavirus data (https://www.ons.gov.uk/peoplepopulationandcommunity/healthandsocialcare/con ditionsanddiseases/articles/coronaviruscovid19/latestinsights) from the ONS and other sources.

- All ONS analysis, summarised in our coronavirus roundup (https://www.ons.gov.uk/peoplepopulationandcommunity/healthandsocialcare/con

- View all coronavirus data
  (https://www.ons.gov.uk/peoplepopulationandcommunity/healthandsocialcare/con
  ditionsanddiseases/datalist).

- Find out how we are working safely in our studies and surveys
  (https://www.ons.gov.uk/news/statementsandletters/ensuringyoursafetyduringcovi
  d19).

Of all CEV people, the majority (89%) were aware that the government shielding guidance for those that are CEV has now ended. Approximately 1 in 5 (22%) reported they were continuing to follow the previous shielding guidance. The majority (68%) of CEV people reported they were no longer shielding but were taking extra precautions. A small proportion of CEV people reported they were not shielding or taking any extra precautions (9%).

The majority of CEV people had left their home in the last seven days (94%). This was statistically significantly (https://www.ons.gov.uk/methodology/methodologytopicsandstatisticalconcepts/uncertaint yandhowwemeasureit#statistical-significance) higher than previous waves (90%, 21 to 26 June 2021 and 89%, 17 to 22 May 2021). Of those who left home in the last seven days, common reasons included going to the shops or pharmacy (79%) and for exercise (58%).

Figure 1: Percentage of clinically extremely vulnerable (CEV) people leaving home in the past seven days is statistically significantly higher than in previous waves

Percentage of CEV people leaving home, England, 11 to 16 October 2021

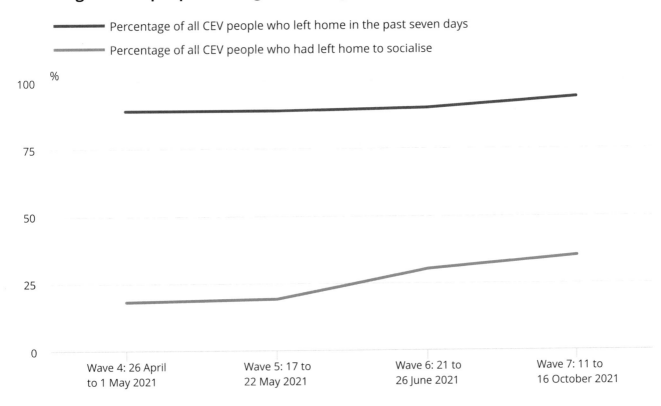

Source: Office for National Statistics – COVID High Risk Group Insights Study

Table 1: Indicators of clinically extremely vulnerable people's behaviours and well-being England, 2021

Indicators of following guidance	Wave 4: 26 April to 1 May 2021	Wave 5: 17 to 22 May 2021	Wave 6: 21 to 26 June 2021	Wave 7: 11 to 16 October 2021
Those who have received two doses of the vaccine[1]	67	86	93	96
Those who reported not leaving the house at all in the last seven days	11	11	10	6
Of those who have left home in the last seven days, those who reported leaving the house to socialise	21	22	33	37
Those who reported that the coronavirus pandemic poses a major or significant risk to their health[2]	41	40	41	46
Those who were very or somewhat worried about the effect of the coronavirus pandemic on their life[2]	53	49	51	47
Those whose well-being and mental health was much or slightly better compared to last month[2]	22	22	20	22

Source: Office for National Statistics – COVID High Risk Group Insights Study

Notes

1. This percentage for wave seven also includes those who have received more than two doses of the vaccine.

2. Well-being questions were not asked to those responding by proxy on behalf of someone else.

3. Well-being of clinically extremely vulnerable people

The average life satisfaction scores of clinically extremely vulnerable (CEV) people were statistically significantly (https://www.ons.gov.uk/methodology/methodologytopicsandstatisticalconcepts/uncertaintyandhowwemeasureit#statistical-significance) lower in those continuing to shield (6.3 out of 10), compared with those not shielding but taking precautions (7.2) and those not shielding and not taking extra precautions (7.5). Average life satisfaction for the general adult population of England was 7.0. For more information, please see Coronavirus and the social impacts on Great Britain: 22 October 2021 (https://www.ons.gov.uk/peoplepopulationandcommunity/healthandsocialcare/healthandwellbeing/bulletins/coronavirusandthesocialimpactsongreatbritain/22october2021). Well-being questions were not asked to those responding by proxy on behalf of someone else.

Figure 2: Life satisfaction was statistically significantly lower in those who were continuing to follow the previous shielding guidance compared to those who were not

Average life satisfaction, by current shielding status, England, 11 to 16 October 2021

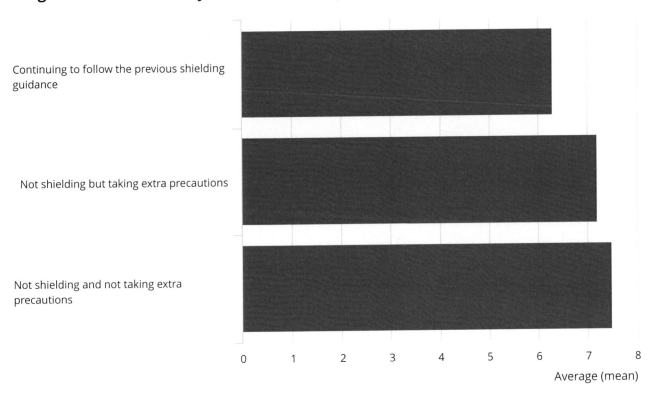

Source: Office for National Statistics – COVID High Risk Group Insights Study

Similar to findings from the previous wave (21 to 26 June 2021), a statistically significant (https://www.ons.gov.uk/methodology/methodologytopicsandstatisticalconcepts/uncertaint yandhowwemeasureit#statistical-significance) higher proportion of CEV people reported feeling lonely often or always, compared with the general adult population of England (10% and 6% respectively). For more information, please see Coronavirus and the social impacts on Great Britain: 22 October 2021 (https://www.ons.gov.uk/peoplepopulationandcommunity/healthandsocialcare/healthandw ellbeing/bulletins/coronavirusandthesocialimpactsongreatbritain/22october2021).

4. Clinically extremely vulnerable people data

Coronavirus and clinically extremely vulnerable people in England (https://www.ons.gov.uk/peoplepopulationandcommunity/healthandsocialcare/conditio nsanddiseases/datasets/coronavirusandclinicallyextremelyvulnerablepeopleinengland) Dataset | Released 2 November 2021
Clinically extremely vulnerable (CEV) people in England during the coronavirus (COVID-19) pandemic from the COVID High Risk Group Insights Study. Includes information on their behaviours and well-being since receiving shielding guidance.

5. Glossary

Clinically extremely vulnerable

People who were identified as clinically extremely vulnerable (CEV) were considered to be at very high risk of severe illness from the coronavirus (COVID-19). Up to 16 February 2021, CEV people were identified either because of a pre-existing condition or based on the clinical judgement of their clinician or GP that they were at higher risk of serious illness if they caught COVID-19.

From 16 February 2021, individuals were still identified as CEV by these routes, but also by the COVID-19 population risk assessment. The NHS identified approximately 2.2 million people as being CEV by clinical condition or clinician's review. A further 1.5 million people were advised to shield through the COVID-19 population risk assessment.

From 15 September 2021, the shielding programme ended in England. People who were previously considered CEV were advised they should follow the national guidance on staying safe and preventing the spread of COVID-19 and may want to consider advice from a health professional on whether additional precautions are right.

More information can be found in Coronavirus Shielded Patient List Summary Totals (https://digital.nhs.uk/data-and-information/publications/statistical/mi-english-coronavirus-covid-19-shielded-patient-list-summary-totals/28-march-2021) and Guidance on shielding and protecting people who are CEV from COVID-19 (https://www.gov.uk/government/publications/guidance-on-shielding-and-protecting-extremely-vulnerable-persons-from-covid-19/guidance-on-shielding-and-protecting-extremely-vulnerable-persons-from-covid-19).

Shielding

From 1 April 2021, the advice to shield paused and from 15 September 2021 the shielding programme ended. Shielding was a voluntary action in which the individual stays in their home or garden as much as possible, except for leaving their household to attend essential medical appointments or for exercise. Guidance during the most recent period of shielding (January to March 2021) included that CEV people:

- can meet one person outdoors from another household for exercise

- should try to stay two metres away from others within their household, especially if they display symptoms of the coronavirus or have been advised to self-isolate

- can still meet with their support bubble

- should try to access services to minimise the need to leave their home, such as food and prescription delivery services

Precautionary guidance

From 1 April 2021 CEV people were advised to take precautions to minimise the risk of exposure to the virus whilst also adhering to the rules in place for everyone. The extra precautions for CEV people include:

- considering whether they and those they are meeting have been vaccinated; they might want to wait until 14 days after everyone's second dose of a COVID-19 vaccine before being in close contact with others

- considering continuing to practice social distancing if that feels right for them and their friends

- asking friends and family to take a rapid lateral flow antigen test before visiting them

- asking home visitors to wear face coverings

- avoiding crowded spaces

The current guidance can be viewed in Guidance on shielding and protecting people who are CEV from COVID-19 (https://www.gov.uk/government/publications/guidance-on-shielding-and-protecting-extremely-vulnerable-persons-from-covid-19/guidance-on-shielding-and-protecting-extremely-vulnerable-persons-from-covid-19).

6. Measuring the data

Survey information

This is the seventh bulletin in this series, with the survey in its current format and using the current data collection methodology. However, it is not directly comparable with wave one and wave two (18 to 30 January 2021 and 22 to 27 February 2021) of this survey because of changes in the shielding population; for more information please see Coronavirus and clinically extremely vulnerable people in England methodology (https://www.ons.gov.uk/peoplepopulationandcommunity/healthandsocialcare/conditionsa nddiseases/methodologies/coronavirusandclinicallyextremelyvulnerablepeopleinenglandme thodology#identifying-clinically-extremely-vulnerable-people). The data in wave one and wave two reflect only clinically extremely vulnerable (CEV) people identified through a clinical condition or clinician's review.

Estimates for wave seven

The data for wave seven were collected between 11 and 16 October 2021. The sample size was 1,025 CEV people and survey weighting was used to weight the sample estimates to provide estimates for the total population of CEV people. For more information on how the estimates have been produced, please see Coronavirus and clinically extremely vulnerable people in England methodology (https://www.ons.gov.uk/peoplepopulationandcommunity/healthandsocialcare/conditionsa nddiseases/methodologies/coronavirusandclinicallyextremelyvulnerablepeopleinenglandme thodology).

Changes to the shielding guidance

From 1 April 2021, CEV people were issued precautionary guidance and still had to follow the national restrictions in place. From 15 September 2021, the shielding programme ended. Waves one to three were collected when shielding was advised, prior to 1 April 2021; any comparisons between wave three or earlier and wave four, five, six or seven should be made with this in mind. Wave seven was collected following the shielding programme in England ending.

7. Strengths and limitations

Information on the strengths and limitations of this survey are available in <u>Coronavirus and clinically extremely vulnerable people in England methodology</u> (<u>https://www.ons.gov.uk/peoplepopulationandcommunity/healthandsocialcare/conditionsa nddiseases/methodologies/coronavirusandclinicallyextremelyvulnerablepeopleinenglandme thodology</u>).

8. Related links

Coronavirus and clinically extremely vulnerable people in England methodology (https://www.ons.gov.uk/peoplepopulationandcommunity/healthandsocialcare/conditio nsanddiseases/methodologies/coronavirusandclinicallyextremelyvulnerablepeopleinen glandmethodology)

Methodology article | Updated 2 November 2021

Latest quality and methodology information on data from the COVID High Risk Group Insights Survey and its use to analyse the behaviours and well-being of clinically extremely vulnerable people.

Coronavirus (COVID-19) latest data and analysis (https://www.ons.gov.uk/peoplepopulationandcommunity/healthandsocialcare/conditio nsanddiseases)

Webpage | Updated as and when data become available

Latest data and analysis on the coronavirus (COVID-19) in the UK and its effect on the economy and society.

Coronavirus (COVID-19) latest insights (https://www.ons.gov.uk/peoplepopulationandcommunity/healthandsocialcare/conditio nsanddiseases/articles/coronaviruscovid19/latestinsights)

Interactive tool | Updated as and when data become available

A live roundup of the latest data and trends about the coronavirus (COVID-19) pandemic from the ONS and other sources.

Coronavirus and clinically extremely vulnerable people in England: 21 to 26 June 2021 (https://www.ons.gov.uk/peoplepopulationandcommunity/healthandsocialcare/conditio nsanddiseases/bulletins/coronavirusandclinicallyextremelyvulnerablepeopleinengland/ 21juneto26june2021)

Bulletin | Released 13 July 2021

Analysis of clinically extremely vulnerable people in England during the coronavirus (COVID-19) pandemic, including their behaviours and mental and physical well-being.

[Coronavirus and shielding of clinically extremely vulnerable people in England: 9 to 16 July 2020
(https://www.ons.gov.uk/peoplepopulationandcommunity/healthandsocialcare/conditionsanddiseases/bulletins/coronavirusandshieldingofclinicallyextremelyvulnerablepeopleinengland/9julyto16july2020)](https://www.ons.gov.uk/peoplepopulationandcommunity/healthandsocialcare/conditionsanddiseases/bulletins/coronavirusandshieldingofclinicallyextremelyvulnerablepeopleinengland/9julyto16july2020)

Bulletin | Released 5 August 2020

Analysis of clinically extremely vulnerable people (the shielding population) in England during the coronavirus (COVID-19) pandemic, including their behaviours and mental and physical well-being.

[Coronavirus (COVID-19) harmonisation guidance (https://gss.civilservice.gov.uk/policy-store/coronavirus-covid-19-harmonisation-guidance/)](https://gss.civilservice.gov.uk/policy-store/coronavirus-covid-19-harmonisation-guidance/)

Webpage | Updated frequently

This page provides harmonisation guidance on how best to collect data about the impact of the coronavirus (COVID-19) pandemic. Users can also find a bank of questions from multiple Office for National Statistics (ONS) surveys related to COVID-19 to be used in other surveys to further support harmonisation and questionnaire development. This bank also provides users with an understanding of what data ONS has in relation to the coronavirus pandemic.

Contact details for this statistical bulletin

Hannah Mason
publicservicesanalysis@ons.gov.uk
Telephone: +44 1633 456979